THE WAY
Made Simple

Mike Dalrymple

This book is not in anyway tied to or associated with any religion, denomination, group, or church. Nor is its purpose to have you give money or join any organization; just the opposite. The goal is to give you a deeper understanding of the force that created our world and his desire for us.

Cover Design: Creative Publishing Book Design
Illustrations by: Natalia Junqueira & Creative Publishing Book Design

ISBN (paperback): 979-8-9994154-3-1
ISBN (hardcover): 979-8-9994154-2-4
ISBN (ebook): 979-8-9994154-1-7

The Bible was written in ancient Greek, which is a dead language. All definitions are from Strong's Numbers and Concordance with Expanded Greek-Hebrew Dictionary.

Dedicated to Megan, Cindy, Kathey, and their families.

He rewards those who earnestly seek him.
Hebrews 11:6

Table of Contents

In the Tanakh, or Old Testament, God has many names, each referring to different aspects of who he is and what he has done. When God spoke to Moses in the burning bush he gave his name as "YHWH" and said, "This is my name forever, the name you shall call me from generation to generation." (Gen. 3:15) To distinguish the name he gave from the others the writers always wrote it in all capital letters as LORD. The name was always held in reverence and rarely spoke out loud. In the New Testament, the writers always use the Greek word for deity unless quoiting the Tanakh. Today we often take his name lightly using phrases such as "OMG" without thought. In keeping with the way it was used in the Old Testament, I have chosen to put it in all capital letters when referring to the persona of God out of respect. I hope it adds rather than distracts from your reading of the book.

Introduction

Today, like every other day, people are born and people die. Your day is coming, and there's not a thing you can do about it. Why are you here? What's the point? What's the purpose? In the end, we all just do the best we can and live each day like a child grabbing as many blocks as possible and stacking them until they fall over.

While you're busy stacking your blocks it's easy to lose your way, especially when happiness turns to heartache and joy to pain. It can make you wonder if you ever knew the way, and what is the point to all of this? Even when things are going well there can be a shallowness in lack of purpose as each day goes by, each joy fades, and we come one day closer to death. If there is a true God where is he? Who is he, why did he put me here, and what does he want? Is there really a "Way" to live? We are born with nothing but our intellect and instincts to find our way. Where do we look? Other people? Religion?

Some people have spent a great deal of time thinking about it in depth, and over the years we have seen many different

concepts. Some are very good written by people of great intellect, and some not so much. Some have even been the basis
for religions. Many have existed for centuries and others are
new. They can give us comfort and even point us toward God,
but all that are written by the hand of man are limited to
the knowledge, wisdom, and intellect of the person writing.
Therefore they will all fall short at some point. Just because
someone has a title doesn't make them right. GOD thinks we're
all pretty special and he's pretty good at saying what he means
and meaning what he says.

There are a lot of different ideas floating around out there,
a lot of different paths going a lot of different directions, and
they can't all be right. What do you believe and why? Many
have taken a belief that makes sense to them and then made
everything else fit with it, right or wrong. Like ignoring the
other side of the coin or finding a way to just make it fit. We
force a square peg in a round hole, or maybe just a slightly oval
one, and we are busy banging away on that hammer because
it "has to fit." We are called his children for a reason; we all
need to grow in knowledge and understanding. When we
stop learning, we stop growing. Where are you on the growth
chart? Have you stopped growing? Are you happy with where
you are? Or perhaps you've even gotten a little shorter lately?
Are you ready to grow or are you afraid to let go and explore
the possibility there may be more, perhaps another side to
the coin you haven't seen or looked at closely enough? Are
you ready for some growing pains? Until you are willing to

let go of everything you thought you knew about God and seek him as he is, you will miss him, along with your purpose in life and the peace that comes with it. It is not up to me or you to define him, who he is, what he has done, or to set his boundaries. You may believe in God, even have a zeal for him, but if you are hanging on to an unchallenged concept of who he is, you can in ignorance miss him altogether. With all the different religions and ideas out there, what are the odds that you are the one who has everything right and have nothing else to learn? Without knowledge and a proper understanding, as with anything in life, you're missing out.

Our place is not to change his Word but to decide if we will allow him to have full control, every time, always, and **especially** when we don't understand. Nobody knows everything, which means everybody's wrong about something. Success in knowing God comes from understanding who we are, and putting GOD in the proper place. In this confusing world, surrounded by ideas and teachings that are not from God, we have to have the understanding and wisdom to confirm what is right, as well as the courage to change what is wrong. If our faith is anchored in the right place, nothing new or different should ever make us uncomfortable, at least for too long. Humility is a necessity for learning, and pride restricts knowledge.

This book was not written to be popular, or just to make people feel good. It was written to bring everyone, no matter their background or beliefs, to a better understanding of who the living GOD is and the way to find joy and purpose in living, as well as dying, by being close to Him. If you can, and if you are ready to better understand and walk a little closer to the Almighty, ready to grow by taking a few minutes to learn The Way a little more perfectly, it doesn't matter if you're a non-believer or a devout disciple. If you're ready then read on, this is for you.

This book follows a logical order but does not have to be read in order. If you feel a need to jump ahead please make sure to read chapter three before doing so.

If you struggle to believe in a God, please read chapter one through three.

If you struggle to believe that Jesus was who Christians say he was, please read chapter two and three along with the appendix.

If you are going to read any other parts of this book, please read chapter three.

If you re a new christian, just along for the ride, or have felt a little flat lately, please make sure to read chapter five.

If you belong to Christ, or thinking about, it please make sure to read chapters six through eight.

If you are active in the world around us, make sure you read chapter nine.

If you have a heart, make sure to read chapter ten.

If you want to know what happens to us when we die, read chapter eleven.

If you want to know more, read chapter twelve.

Before you leave the book on the self make *absolutely sure* to read chapter four.

Chapter One

The Way to GOD

"Anyone who comes to him must believe that he exists and that he rewards those who earnestly seek him." (Heb 11:6) Why? Why would any intelligent person believe in a deity? With all the pain, problems, injustices, and death we all face, why would *any* deity allow it, let alone a God who loves us?

First of all, to be honest, we have to allow for the fact of what we bring on ourselves: war, greed, hatred, and everything that comes with it. Then there's all the pollution of the air, water, and soil and what that does to our bodies. Not to mention the way we travel, strapping ourselves into big pieces of steel and flying down the road missing one another by inches, or flying in big aluminum tubes breathing oxygen from a tank. And then we want to blame God for our problems? As though it's his fault and he should stop us? It's truly amazing we do as well as we do! But let's face it—that doesn't account for everything. Sometimes things just happen and death comes to all, which means if there is a God, he must look at things differently than we do. That shouldn't surprise us; in fact it's by nature a necessity. Our knowledge is limited to only a small amount of what is present and what came before, with the vast majority of our information coming from someone else. A creator on the other hand would have first-hand knowledge of all that is now, was, and is to come. That alone would cause him to see things differently than we do. A creator would also have a full understanding of things we can't see or even imagine: other dimensions, the spirit world, what happens to us when we die—the list is long. That by necessity would cause actions on his part we couldn't begin to understand. So with just our limited knowledge of the world, both present and past, can we see and understand enough to believe in a deity, a creator?

An apostle of Jesus named Paul, writing to people in Rome who had some rather strange concepts of god, not too long after the death of Jesus put it this way: "For since the creation of the world God's invisible qualities—his eternal power and divine nature—have been clearly seen, being understood from what has been made, so that people are without excuse." (Rom 1:20) Science has come to some undeniable and proven conclusions or laws. The first law of energy, or thermodynamics, states "Energy cannot be created or destroyed, it can only be changed from one form to another."[1] Or, simply stated, something cannot come from nothing. If you take a box of any size with nothing in it, and seal it up so nothing can get in or out it doesn't matter how long you wait; when you open it up again, what would you expect to find? Without the presence of an outside force, nothing would exist. Period.

The second law of thermodynamics states that in all energy exchanges, if no energy enters or leaves the system, the potential energy of the state will always be less than that of the initial state.[2] Or to put it another way, without an outside force everything winds down, never the other way around. Your economy car will never become a luxury car on its own. In fact, both will eventually fall apart, and neither will run without constantly being feed of some type of fuel. Both this world and the life on it are amazing and extremely complex. Every answer that teams of intelligent people struggle to find reveals a long list of other questions. Any chance of this happening without an outside force is nonexistent. You can take a deck of cards and throw them in the air as many times as you like, but they will never come down with all fifty-two stacked one upon another arranged in a house of cards. That only happens with an intelligent design, and a very steady hand. Now, think how much

---

[1] Quote from Albert Einstein.
[2] Generally credited to Rudolf Clausius.

more complex the world is arranged than a house of cards. There just is no way all of this came about without an extremely intelligent and powerful outside force.

If there was a massive explosion at an auto factory would anyone expect to see fully assembled cars scattered around, programmed to run with keys in the ignition and ready to go? Have you ever known anything to be created from an explosion? Except maybe a hole in the ground? What is the possibility that you could assemble anything, let alone a car or truck, from an explosion? Yet we have pretty much come to a universal conclusion that all that exists came from the Big Bang, a massive explosion. Our bodies, our intellect, the world, the universe, and beyond, are so far beyond the complexity of a car they can't even be compared. The whole of the universe, all that exists, with everything perfectly balanced, all the complexities of life, all assembled from an explosion *without* an intelligent force behind it? Does that even make sense??

Let's change gears for a minute. How many diets have you seen come and go over the years? How many different diets do you think you could find online right now? It seems as though they are about as numerous as the stars in the sky. Most of them were made by intelligent people, often highly educated doctors, or dietitians, with many years of training, and yet they often contradict each other. Many of them don't work for everyone, and some sound good only to find out later that they can actually cause health problems. The diet given by GOD through Moses in Leviticus 11:1-23 and Deuteronomy 14:3-21 for the new nation of Israel was very specific. It was different from any other diet Moses had known. Without today's knowledge or any training, Moses gave them a diet in 1300-1400BC that pretty much all doctors, and those that study the effects of diet and health, agree is good for pretty much everybody—even today. Even those who want to qualify certain parts of the diet will tell you that it's certainly not bad for you. Just think about how much more important your diet would become if you couldn't get a thermometer to cook with! While it's not part of the New Covenant we live by today, the only way that this could be possible is that Moses received it from a loving and knowledgeable Creator.

"How foolish can you be? You turn things upside down! Shall the potter be considered as equal with the clay? Should the created thing say of the one who made it, 'He did not make me?' Can the pot say of the potter, 'He knows nothing, he has no understanding?' Does a jar ever say, 'The potter who made me is stupid?'" (Isa. 29:16 author's composite of NLT, NSAB, and NIV.) We all do it. We make a god of our choosing. We create a god the way we perceive him, or would like him to be. Then we ask him, "Why did you make me this way?" Or "Why did it happen to me?" Without realizing it we have created a god just like the ancients who carved a god out of wood or stone. We have created a god in our image rather than the other way around,[3] and in doing so we live in the dark without understanding, missing the greatest opportunity life has to offer. We

---

[3] From the video series; "Does God Exist" by John Clayton.

create a god using our logic, a few excerpts from the Bible, or a book that speaks to us. We create a god from our feelings, one we understand, and are comfortable with. Then we put him in a box and then either set him on a shelf, cast him aside, or carry him around with us like a charm on a chain, one we can take out and rub when needed. Once locked in he lives there forever because to make a change would be too uncomfortable. Just because we have come to a clear logical perception of who he is doesn't mean we're correct—chances are we're not. We can even logically deny his very existence simply because of the perception we've created of him.

Truth is, none of us are right. The more you come to know, and the more accurate you are, the more you realize how little you know, and just how truly vast the true God really is. If you ever get to a point where you think you know God extremely well you are either wrong or like an infant, just beginning to learn. It's only when the door is cracked open and light comes into a room that we see all the shadows and dark places that exist. A little bit of light only gives a little bit of information. To find the true God we have to be willing to let go of the god we have created and boxed up, not just once, but all the time. Tear open and discard the box, let go of the fear of what you might find, and let Him speak through His Word. Let HIM form you, not the other way around. Above all keep an open mind; look at things you are sure of as if you've never seen them before. Seek the truth at **any cost**, because a lie is worthless, and be ready to learn because you never know when, or just how, he will show himself.

10

Chapter Two
The Way to Belief

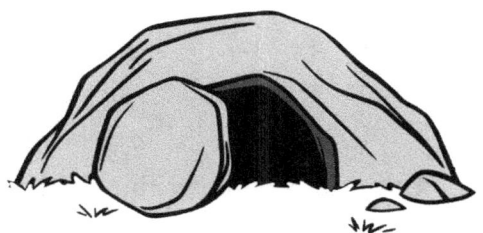

So how do you find GOD? A lot of people over the years have had some really good ideas and there are some really good books on how to live and draw close to the divine, as well as any number of religions all with different teachings. Which one is right? It would seem that a God who was capable of creating life, heaven, and earth would do something special to make his words stand out, send up a flare so to speak, and say **"HERE I AM"**—He did.

The book printed far more than any other presents the man we've all heard of, Jesus. His DNA was created by GOD himself and planted in a young virgin, then later as a man GOD's Spirit came down and lived in him making him God on earth. He teaches GOD's desire for man in a way that no one else could or can. He made remarkable claims and backed them up with undeniable miracles. By taking on everything that we have done that has separated us from GOD and dying as a sacrifice, he has made a way for us to start over and draw close to GOD. What better way to reach out to mankind than to become one of us? If true, it is the biggest flare the world has ever seen!! It would also make sense that the calendar would stop and start over with him.

Imagine you found an ancient book that had accurately described events that happened in the future. Would you find that interesting, want to know more? Suppose someone accurately described Hitler five hundred years before he was born, where he would be born at, the terrible things he would do, even what would happen at the end. Wouldn't it make you think and wish that someone would have listened and done something? How much more someone from a completely different world and time coming to the earth to reach out and enlighten mankind? And suppose he were talked about repeatedly by many writers for centuries before he came? That would certainly make him someone worth listening to.

There has been only one man whose entire life was foretold by numerous people going back as far as 1,400 years before he was born. That someone would announce him, the unusual way he would come into the world, and where, the way he would teach, the things he would do, how he would be received, the way he would be killed, even the exact amount of money he would be betrayed for. That he would accomplish creating a new covenant between GOD and mankind, and that his body would not decay in the ground nor in some tomb somewhere.

That's too much to just be a coincidence. There are well over three hundred descriptions of Jesus going back hundreds of years before he was born. Over sixty of them are direct prophecies written by different men at different times in history; sixteen of them are in the Appendix. Take just a minute to flip over to page 167 and check them out along with the mathematician's statements as to the odds, and when high odds can become impossible. Isaiah chapter 53 describes his life and purpose with certainty, almost like the sun coming up tomorrow, not getting even one thing wrong seven hundred years before he was born! How could this be possible? What are the chances??

Jewish leaders today teach people that the Messiah is still to come. GOD, Gabriel, and Daniel all tell a different story. The angel Gabriel tells Daniel the times and order of things, talks about the rebuilding of Jerusalem and the temple, and then says, "The Anointed One will be put to death and will have nothing. The people of the ruler who will come will destroy the city and the sanctuary. The end will come like a flood: War will continue until the end, and desolations have been decreed." (Dan. 9:26) God speaking through Gabriel was clear that the Messiah would come before the City and the temple were destroyed in AD 70. In effect, making Jesus the Messiah.

It is a historical fact that Jesus lived and that he was put to death on a cross.[1] It is also undeniable that his body disappeared

---

[1] Historian Flavius Josephus in the Antiquities of the Jews Book 18:63 & 20:200

just days after his death. It's obvious those responsible for his death wouldn't take it, which leaves his followers. As many as five hundred and twenty people, many named, claim to have seen a resurrected Jesus after his death. Some saw him suddenly appear and also leave the same way, a number of them at the same time. Many claim not only to have seen him but also to have touched him, and even eaten with him. All of them alive at the same time and shortly after his death. This would make for a very large conspiracy if it were not true. This might be possible if there was something to be gained. The fact is though, none of them "cashed in." In fact, most suffered and were willing to face a painful death rather than deny what they saw. Skeptics claim it's too far-fetched, or that since the Bible was written before the printing press it can't be trusted. If you can see a creator with the power to create heaven and earth as well as put life on it, wouldn't it be a rather small thing for him to create someone special to reach out to mankind and then edit a book and make sure it survived intact—just as the Bible has?

Often taken for granted and set aside, the Bible is an extremely unique piece of literature, there is nothing else like it. It is made up of sixty-six different "books." The Old Testament comprises the same material as the Tanakh[2] (tuh-naak) or Hebrew Bible. There are thirty-nine books in the Old Testament; in the Tanakh they are grouped together to

---

[2] For more information on the history of the Jewish people and the coming of the Messiah visit https://hebrew-streams.org/.

make twenty-four. The Old Testament is generally divided into four divisions: the first five are Law, twelve are History, five are Poetry, and then the Prophets, consisting of five major and twelve minor. The Tanakh is divided into three divisions: The first five of the law are called the Torah. The prophets are called the Neviim, (ne-ve-em) and they are divided into four former, three latter, and one minor. Then there are eleven Writings called the Ketuvim (ke-tu-vim). They all teach us how GOD acts and reacts, even today; "I am the LORD, and I do not change." (Mal 3:6 NLT)

Of the twenty-seven books in the New Covenant, or New Testament, the first four tell the story of Jesus. His birth, his life, what he did, and what he taught, as well as his death, burial, and resurrection in what is referred to as the "Gospel" or "Good News." The next book is about the creation of the church, or the "called out." How it began, first with the Jews and then throughout the whole world. How even today we can be forgiven for everything we've done, start a relationship with the one true and living GOD, and become part of something that transcends this life. Then there are twenty-one letters written to various people and churches about applying the teachings of Jesus to everyday life, no matter when, or where we live. The last book is prophetic, written in symbolic language about what is to happen leading to the end of time and the judgment. The Bible was written over a period of about 1500 years, by at least thirty-nine different people, yet all the different writings, or books, flow together as one with one central theme: that of a Creator and his desire for mankind. It's all in there. How to find the true GOD, understand him, and build a relationship with him. How to find peace, joy, and love, as well as how to get through the hard times. How to talk the talk as well as walk the walk. Where we came from and where we're headed. It does not change with the times. "Jesus Christ[3] is the same yesterday and today and forever." (Heb 13:8) You just have to stop, look, and listen.

---

[3] Christ #5547 Christos (khris-tos'); from NT:5548; anointed, i.e. the Messiah, an epithet of Jesus:

Chapter Three

The Way to Understanding

"For since the creation of the world God's invisible qualities—his eternal power and divine nature—have been clearly seen, being understood from what has been made, so that people are without excuse." (Rom 1:20) If we can see GOD through his creation, or handiwork, wouldn't it follow that his words for the world would reflect the same handiwork or personality?

From the earliest times, man has noticed a duality to life. Light and dark, male and female, hot and cold, pain and joy, even and odd, happy and sad, over and over again, even good and evil. In the same way, the Bible completes itself by showing both sides of the coin, and sometimes even the sides. Just as the two sides of a coin can-not be separated, so also the two sides of GOD's teaching can-not be separated, and one is just as important as the other. The same fingerprint found on creation is found in the Bible. To fully understand the whole, one must understand both sides and how they complement and support each other. This, while giving a complete picture of the subject, makes it all the more important that we do as Paul told the younger Timothy "Do your best to present yourself to God as one approved, a worker who does not need to be ashamed and who correctly handles the word of truth." (2 Tim 2:15)

The Bible is like no other book written. If you look at just one side you literally can make the Bible say anything you want. Studying the Bible with preconceived ideas will never give you a clear picture of what it says. If you study to prove yourself right, you will—every time, no matter the subject. This is the reason we have so much division in religion, with so many people teaching and believing so many different things while all reading the same book. It is imperative we know all sides of any subject to understand GOD's Word, to "correctly handle the word of truth." Just because one subject, or one side of a coin, is emphasized in one place or even many, it does not negate the other side or make it any less true. Although one side may be emphasized in different places, like pieces of a puzzle they are both part of the whole. You simply **can-not** take your pick on which verse, or which side of the coin, you want to believe and disregard another. When you pick up one, the other is attached as well.

Jesus said, "I did not come to bring peace, but a sword." (Matt 10:34) Just like a coin has two sides it takes two opposing sides to come together in order to make a blade. The sword that Jesus brings has many effects on the lives of those who choose to pick it up and follow him. It is extremely sharp and it does not dull with time or usage. "For the word of God is alive and active. Sharper than any double-edged sword, it penetrates even to dividing *soul and spirit*"[1] (Heb 4:12) Why double-edged? If you are ready to defend yourself you need to be acquainted with and know how to use both sides. They are both needed and equally important in order to accomplish the task Jesus has given us. If you are going around swinging a single-edge sword, it may look cool, but it is not complete and not the one from GOD. Guns, poisons, and explosives, are all powerful, but they can-not accomplish the task at hand. This sword is alive and has a purpose other than destruction, which is to penetrate deep into the soul and separate the spirit, remove that which is diseased, and bring a new spirit to life. No matter which side you may have chosen or for whatever reason, a single-edge blade is not up to the task and will fail you. The sword that Jesus brings is complete and is the only thing that can defend us. It is what Jesus used to defend himself when attacked by Satan, and it is the only thing that Satan respects, therefore it allows us to do the same. "Jesus said to him, "Away from me, Satan! For it is written: 'Worship the Lord your God, and serve

---

[1] soul:# 5590; psuche (psoo-khay') (from # 5594 to breath); breath, i.e. (by implication) spirit, abstractly or concretely (the animal sentient principle only; thus distinguished on the one hand from [2]#4151 (spirit) which is the rational and immortal soul.)

him only." (Matt 4:10) Just as Jesus knew and spoke the whole truth, in order to be his disciples we have to strive to do the same. Without the Word we are defenseless.

Believing something, even honestly, does not make it right, any more than running a stop sign out of ignorance relieves you of the potential consequences. Hanging on to a false belief or worse yet, choosing to be ignorant can have dire effects not only for ourselves but also for those for who listen to us. It's like driving blind. Some are afraid of what they might learn, but the truth is that we should be more afraid of NOT knowing or not learning. Ignorance won't work with most aspects of life, and it won't work with GOD. We have the "perfect law of liberty" (James 1:25) open to all of us. "**ALL** Scripture is God-breathed and is useful for teaching, rebuking, correcting and training in righteousness, so that the servant of God may be thoroughly equipped for every good work." (II Tim 3:16-17 emphasis mine) Always read GOD's Word with an open mind. *Never* put an interpretation on one Scripture that violates another, and always use the clear verse to give meaning to the difficult verse, never the other way around. It is only when we empty ourselves and let all the pieces fit together that the picture can become clear. It is then that GOD makes himself known and fills our heart.

Some have said that the Bible is difficult to understand. This is no doubt true if you understand it the way some do. But if you open your heart and mind to GOD and let him speak through his Word to you, a complete picture emerges, and your world changes. GOD and his Word are one and can-not be separated. Close either one of them out, and you are lost. "The Word became flesh and made his dwelling among us. We have seen his glory, the glory of the one and only Son, who came from the Father, full of grace and truth." (John 1:14) When it comes to duality, Jesus was the ultimate. While physicality being a man in every way like us, his spirit was that of GOD making him God in every way. Just like God the Father, it's in his actions, and it's in his teaching. Of all the dualities of life we can see Jesus came teaching the most profound and important, that we are both physical and spiritual. Also, just as important, as long as we're alive, one affects the other. Your experiences, what you have done and do, has and will always affect your spirit, who you are, how you look at things, and how you think. It is also true that your spirit and the way you think will always affect what you do.

Many of the Jews of Jesus' day, especially the leaders, failed to understand this and missed out. They were so focused on the physical law of the Torah that they missed the closeness to GOD that comes with living under the New Covenant promised in Jeremiah 31:31 and the superiority[2] of being in a spiritual

---

[2] "But the ministry Jesus has received is as superior to theirs as the covenant of which he is mediator is superior to the old one, and it is founded on better promises. For if there had been nothing wrong with that first covenant, no place would have been sought for another... "The time is coming, declares the Lord, when I will make a new covenant... I will put my laws in their minds and write them on their hearts." Heb 8:6-10 & Jer 31: 31-34

kingdom. Under the physical law given by GOD the temple was the dwelling place of the LORD, and it was there that the priests were to offer sacrifices for atonement. Under Rabbinic Judaism they decided the temple, the priesthood, and sacrifices commanded in the Torah would all come to an end. Under the spiritual law of Jesus the Messiah, it's only natural that all three still remain. The temple is still the dwelling place of the LORD; "Do you not know that you are God's temple and that God's Spirit dwells in you?" (1 Cor 3:16 ESV) The priesthood; "But you are a chosen people, a royal priesthood, a holy nation, Gods special possession."(1 Peter 2:9) and a sacrifice to end all sacrifices; "We have been made holy through the sacrifice of the body of Jesus Christ once for all." (Heb 10:10) It is not by coincidence that in AD 70, shortly after the death of Jesus Christ, the temple in Jerusalem was destroyed, the priesthood scattered, and animal sacrifices ended. After centuries, atonement under the Torah had ended and was no longer possible. The LORD did not abandon them; they abandoned him. The creation of Rabbinic Judaism, with its formality of liturgy, the traditions of the Mishnah, and prayers offered to God, do not remove sin. The Torah is clear; without a sacrifice, sin remains. "For the life of a creature is in the blood, and I have given it to you to make atonement for yourselves on the altar; it is the blood that makes atonement for one's life" (Lev. 17:11) It is also not a coincidence that there has not been another prophet after Jesus, over two thousand years ago! Nor will there be. "But even if we or an angel from heaven should preach a gospel other than

the one we preached to you, let them be under God's curse!"
(Gal 1:8) Unfortunately, most Jews are still missing out today;
way too many are trying to hang on to a past that is long gone,
and thereby missing the future that GOD wants for them. If
you're Jewish, it doesn't matter if you're secular, ultra-orthodox,
or somewhere in between; you can once again become chosen
of the LORD and be part of his royal priesthood, worship in
the temple, have your sins washed away through the blood of
the Messiah, and become redeemed under the New Covenant.
"The promise is for you and your children and for all who are
far off—for all whom the Lord our God will call" (Acts 2:39)

"These people come near to me with their mouth and honor
me with their lips, but their hearts are far from me. Their worship
of me is based on merely human rules they have been taught" (Isa
29:13 also Matt 15:8-9) The Mishnah, and later the Talmuds,
are the works of men over many years, roughly from AD 90 to
as late as AD 600. The Catholic church has had as many as three
hundred councils; however, today it recognizes only twenty-
one of them, from 325 to 1965. There are over thirty thousand
Christian denominations with their own teachings worldwide
that have sprung from the Reformation movement beginning
in 1517. Then we have the New Age movement, philosophy
based partly on Scripture and ancient religions. From the Jews
who met at Yavneh in AD 90 to the latest New Age book, all of
these are mostly rules and ideals taught by men. Some are good,
some a little strange, but they all want you to believe that they
are of God and have a better insight than the others.

Mankind in general seems to find it necessary to interpret God for others. Once a church or institution is established we take ownership and resist change. After Jesus raised Lazarus from the dead the Jewish leaders, called the Sanhedrin, called a meeting and it was said "What are we to do? For this man performs many signs. If we let him go on like this, everyone will believe in him, and the Romans will come and take away both our place and our nation." (John 11:47-48 ESV) Notice it's "*our* place" and "*our* nation." Because of pride, they insisted on hanging on to the old ways rather than change. We should all learn from those early Jewish leaders because pride is something that affects all of us, not just others. Making a change in what we have come to believe can be challenging at best, and often very difficult to do. However, if GOD is to be the anchor in our life and we are to grow in Him, we have no other choice but to be ready to learn and also change, since his Word does not. Can you imagine how hard it was for Peter and the early Jewish disciples to change and allow Gentiles into the fellowship of the church? These are people that they had been taught from early childhood to look down on and have nothing to do with. However, they had walked with Jesus and had learned to follow him, even when they didn't yet understand. To be a disciple of Jesus, we have to do the same. We must learn to submit and be ready to change when needed and not get hung up with pride. If we have the correct attitude it's His way, not ours. If we're in the right church it's His, not ours. Our beliefs are not to be our anchor—the Word of GOD is. Pride is hard to overcome, but overcoming is exactly what's required of us.[3] Both sides of the coin are equally true and important—we were created both physical and spiritual. Denying that Jesus requires anything physical of us is just as wrong and devastating as denying the Spirit. One always affects the other and they can-not be separated. Deny one and you miss both. Rules and philosophies made by men will not put you in a relationship with GOD, and they will not save you.

---

[3] "He who overcomes will inherit all this, and I will be his God and he will be my son." Rev 21:7-8

Chapter Four

The Way to Salvation

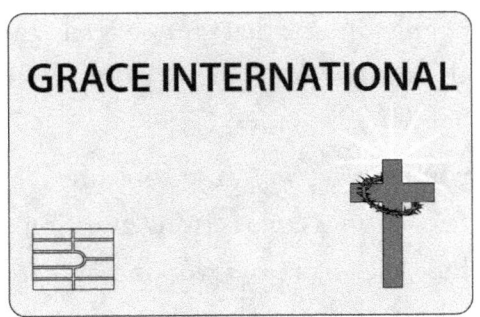

"If we claim to be without sin, we deceive ourselves and the truth is not in us." (1 John 1:8) Let's face it, we've all messed up at one time or another. I know I sure have, and I see it in others too. Only you, and perhaps a few others, know what condemns you, but you know it's there, and GOD does too. Existing across time gives him a good memory. Like Humpty-Dumpy once the words have been spoken or the deeds done, and we fall off that wall, there is simply no way to take it back or make it the same again. Sure we try to learn from our mistakes and do better the next time, but the mistake remains. What seemed like a good idea at the moment, satisfied a deep desire, or just slipped out in an instant has now separated us from GOD and condemned us. "For the wages of sin is death, but the gift of God is eternal life in Christ Jesus our Lord." (Rom 6:23) If we desire to make things right with GOD, and accept his gift, we have to do it on his terms. What you think doesn't matter. What you believe, or what seems to be logical, doesn't matter. What I or anyone else tells you, does, or says, it just doesn't matter. Neither you nor I can put Humpty back together again, only the one that created it all can do that, and his are the only words that matter. It's only by his grace that he has made a way back to him.

Suppose you were to walk into someone's house and see a puzzle sitting over on a table missing a section. So naturally you ask how long they had been working on it, to which they respond "Oh, I put it together seven or eight years ago" You think to yourself, *It's been sitting here seven or eight years unfinished?* Holding back your surprise you ask,"What happened to the missing pieces? Did you lose them?" They respond "Oh no, they are in the box sitting over on the shelf. I just don't like them. I put a few in awhile back, but it didn't feel right, so I took them out. Isn't it beautiful though? It brings me such joy." Might you think they are also missing a few pieces? So why do we do the same thing with God's Word? All the pieces need to fit together and be in place to be complete. We have all the pieces available, and yet we just decide to leave a few in the book sitting on the shelf, preferring one over another. There are many things spoken of throughout the Bible that save us, *grace* is the table on which they rest. "For it is by grace you have been saved, through faith—and this is not from yourselves, it is the gift of God—not by works, so that no one can boast. For we are God's handiwork, created in Christ Jesus to do good works, which God prepared in advance for us to do." (Eph 2:8-10) It is only by the grace of GOD through your belief, or faith in him to do as he promised, that he offers you the gift of forgiveness. That which Christ paid for so you can be close to him, and be saved from your mistakes because he believes in you. He loves you. You are his workmanship, and he takes pride in you. He knows you can do better and he has plans for you, things you were created and prepared for, good works, things no one else can do as good as you. He knows exactly what you are capable of. He has a way for you to live, and a way for you to succeed, if only you are willing to humble yourself, put him first, listen, and trust him. And we all know it's not because we deserve it. "But God demonstrates his own love for us in this: While we were still sinners, Christ died for us." (Rom 5:8) His grace is available to you not because you're good enough, it's available to you because you're not good enough.

But what is grace? The Bible was written in ancient Greek, so from the Greek bible dictionary, Strong's, we have this definition; *Grace*: #5485 charis (khar'-ece); graciousness (as gratifying), of manner or act (abstract or concrete; literal, figurative or spiritual; especially the divine influence upon the heart, and its reflection in the life; including gratitude): from #5463; chairo (khah'-ee-ro); a primary verb; to be "cheerful," i.e. calmly happy or well-off; impersonally, especially as salutation (on meeting or parting), be well:" A lot of people misunderstand and misuse the word *grace.* By definition, it's quite literally when GOD's graciousness, an undeserved gift of forgiveness, has a divine influence on the heart and is reflected in our life in the way of gratitude, with a cheerful happiness. It comes from the word *cheerful* and carries the idea with it of being calm, happy, and well-off.

It takes at least two for grace to exist: one to give and one to receive. It can not be forced on anyone; if it were it wouldn't be grace. It's like if you went out to dinner with friends and had a glass or two of wine. On the way home, a car pulls out of nowhere right in front of you. In the accident, it just so happens that a child was killed. It also turns out you were one step over the line. Just by the slightest of margins you are over the legal limit and have broken the law. It winds up on the news, the public is outraged, and the DA promises the maximum sentence with the maximum fine. However, the parents of the child gracefully choose not to prosecute if you admit wrong-doing and apologize. There will be no jail time, no fine, and no record on file. That's grace. If you refuse it, question it, stand up for your rights, proclaim your innocence that it wasn't your fault, and try to bargain or change the conditions, that's pride, maybe even borderline stupidity. GOD's grace is also conditional, remember we "have been saved *through* faith." In the same way, "Therefore, there is now no condemnation for those who are in Christ Jesus." (Rom. 8:1) So, if your debt is to be paid, you have to be **IN** Christ Jesus; there is simply no other way to receive his grace but to "clothe yourself" with Christ. (Gal 3:27) To let pride, or anything else, get in the

way of meeting the one condition of receiving his grace seems
to me would be one step over the line, and just plain stupid.

There are a lot of smart people and great philosophies, but
if anyone tells you there are many paths to God, it is obvious
they don't know the path to God. Jesus does. He is the only one
who lived sinless because he had the spirit of GOD in everything
he said and everything he did. The only one who died for you,
and the only one who rose again. The only one that still lives,
and the only way to the true and living GOD. "Jesus answered,
"I am the way and the truth and the life. No one comes to the
Father except through me." (John 14:6) His grace is an amazing
gift that is offered to all, but not accepted by all. To those who
accept it, take hold of it, and allow it to influence their heart,
it changes their life. To those that ignore it and turn away, it's
like a Christmas present that sits unopened, year after year,
just waiting to be opened. You know GOD could've made the
conditions for salvation anything he wanted to, but only by his
grace, he made it so easy that anyone, at any time, can receive
it. No pilgrimage required or payment needed. The only test is
if you are ready to humble yourself, close off man's teaching, put
away your pride, and open your heart to His words, His truth.

There has probably been more disagreement and twisting
of God's Word to make our ideas fit, flat-out ignoring the other
side of the coin on the subject of salvation than any other.
Most people have been taught and have come to focus on one
side or the other and unless this is all new to you, there is a
chance that includes you. Rather than tossing out this book or

deleting it, along with the author, I am asking you once again to be open to both sides and *all* Scriptures. Not preferring one over another, but to consider how all of the pieces fit and work together. It doesn't matter how you got here; what matters is how you go forward. GOD's Word is his alone; changing it will not end well. Know that if our interpretation of one verse contradicts or causes you to subjugate or twist another, you are not understanding either. They all come from the same place and are all equally important. "All Scripture is God-breathed and is useful for teaching, rebuking, correcting and training in righteousness, so that the servant of God may be thoroughly equipped for every good work." (2 Tim 3:16-17)

"For God so loved the world that he gave his one and only Son, that whoever believes[1] in him shall not perish but have eternal life." (John 3:16) When Jesus says "whoever believes in him," it means more than just an acknowledgment that Jesus exists; it also by definition carries with it a willingness to entrust one's self to him, to have *faith* in him. "He was delivered over to death for our sins and was raised to life for our justification.[2] Therefore, since we have been justified[3] through faith, we have peace with God through our Lord Jesus Christ, through whom

---

[1] Believe #4100 pisteuo (pist-yoo'-o); to have faith; by implication, to entrust especially one's spiritual well-being to Christ.
[2] Justification #1347 dikaiosis (dik-ah'-yo-sis); acquittal (for Christ's sake): from NT:1344
[3] Justified #1344 dikaioo (dik-ah-yo'-o); to render (i.e. show or regard as) just or innocent:

we have gained access by faith into this grace in which we now stand. And we boast in the hope of the glory of God." (Rom 4:25-5:2) It is only through our belief and faith in Jesus Christ, believing that he died to take away sin and was raised to sit in heaven, that we can have peace with GOD and gain access to his grace. Find faith—find grace; no faith—no grace.

There are many other powerful Scriptures on the importance of an active belief and faith. It is the necessary first step without which no other steps can be made. "And without faith it is impossible to please God, because anyone who comes to him must believe that he exists and that he rewards those who earnestly seek him." (Heb 11:6) You can't go without or skip over it. Many people look good on the outside, do wonderful things, know the scriptures well, and even preach and teach with power, but inside their heart is not right with GOD. Jesus put it this way: "You are like whitewashed tombs, which look beautiful on the outside but on the inside are full of the bones of the dead and everything unclean. In the same way, on the outside you appear to people as righteous but on the inside you are full of hypocrisy and wickedness." (Matt 23:27-28) (Have you ever noticed this always applies to others and never to us?) I absolutely do not want to upset or offend anyone; however, it is critical that we make sure that all verses fit together and that we do not take shortcuts when it comes to understanding the way to salvation. The Bible is clear that letting Jesus into our life, and having belief and faith, is important. So important that many people today have put all their emphasis there, teaching that you just need to pray and "Let Jesus come into your heart." By itself, it's a true enough statement, but the Bible never uses it as a condition of salvation; in fact, that phrase is not even found in the Bible at all. There are many good people who have been taught to put all their focus there, and some proclaim emphatically that's all you need. Jesus and the apostles taught differently—that it's only one side of the coin.

Just before he left the earth Jesus told the apostles "Go into all the world and preach the gospel to all creation. Whoever believes and is baptized will be saved, but whoever does not believe will be condemned." (Mark 16:15-16) There are many pieces of the puzzle that come together to make an amazing picture of a Creator reaching out, not just to a few, but to all of his creation. Jesus allowed himself to be mocked, beaten, tortured, humiliated, and put to death on a cross so that the picture might be complete. It is completely within his right to demand whatever he chooses of us, and yet he brings it all down to these two things, first to have belief, and then to be baptized. The changing of the heart and the answer of our heart to GOD. Two sides of the same coin, both important, both commanded by Jesus. Why should we make one any more or less important than the other? Jesus didn't. Some want to make belief and putting Jesus in your heart more important while others want to make baptism more important, teaching that as long as you were baptized it doesn't matter if you knew why or what was in your heart. Jesus explained what he meant when he told a ruler named Nicodemus: "Jesus replied, "Very truly

I tell you, no one can see the kingdom of God unless they are born again." "How can someone be born when they are old?" Nicodemus asked. "Surely they cannot enter a second time into their mother's womb to be born!" Jesus answered, "Very truly I tell you, no one can enter the kingdom of God unless they are born of water and the Spirit." (John 3:3-5)

They were under a physical law and being born of the Spirit was something entirely new that Nicodemus didn't understand. Being born of water was easy; everyone understood exactly what Jesus was referring to. Immersion was required under the Tanakh, or in the Old Testament, in a number of instances, and John the Baptist had been preaching and baptizing, drawing crowds for some time, perhaps as long as two and a half years. Everybody around had heard about John's teaching, and many were baptized by John. Saying that everybody alive is born of water, and this was what Jesus was talking about, is trying to put a square peg in a round hole—it doesn't fit. It doesn't fit either in the sentence nor in the teachings of Jesus or with what the other Scriptures teach. It also doesn't fit with what Jesus did; not only was Jesus baptized, but he also had his disciples baptize all those who wished to become disciples. "Jesus was gaining and baptizing more disciples than John—although in fact it was not Jesus who baptized, but his disciples." (John 4:1-2)

It wasn't until recent times that some have taken the idea that amniotic fluid was associated with water and tied to a physical birth. There is no reference of it in the Bible, nor is there any reference to the idea anywhere in the time period.

In fact, we don't even use that phrase today to describe all physical births, and never have. If you have to have somebody tell you what it means; there is a good chance it doesn't mean what they are telling you. The idea that everybody needs to be born of the flesh is nonsensical and simply not what he's talking about. Even as Jesus continued on the *whole point* of what he is teaching is that being born of the flesh has nothing at all to do with it—nothing. He tells Nicodemus that "Flesh gives birth to flesh" (John 3:6) The birth that Jesus is talking about is different. Being born of water is part of something we all must decide to do. Nicodemus was physically born into a physical kingdom; and yet Jesus tells him that he must now be born of water as well as the Spirit to enter into a spiritual kingdom. From now on all of us who make the choice to be in the kingdom are "born again" by "water and spirit." Peter had been a disciple of John the Baptist as had others in the group. Peter was there and understood exactly what Jesus meant. When guided by the Holy Spirit he said "Baptism,[4] which now saves you, not by removing dirt from your body, but as a response to God from a clean conscience." (1 Pet. 3:21 NLT) Peter was just as clear as Jesus was; we need to stop thinking of baptism as just a physical act of the flesh, a ceremony, a ritual, or some sort of sign. Rather we need to see it for what it is; our response

---

[4] Baptism #907 baptizo (bap-tid'-zo); to immerse, submerge; to make overwhelmed (i.e. fully wet); used only in the new testament of ceremonial ablution, especially of the ordinance of Christian baptism. Required for proselyte to Judaism (Yeb. 47a; Gerim i.)

in submitting to Jesus in faith, a new birth, a turning point in our life, and a direct commandment of Jesus.

They were all quite familiar with the act of baptism, or immersion, as an act of purification. It was commanded in the Law and tradition in a variety of situations, including converting to Judaism. Often referred to as a *mikvah*, there are a variety of words used in Hebrew to describe it. Peter and his contemporaries were very familiar with these Hebrew words. Peter, writing in Greek, uses the word *baptizo*, meaning to immerse as someone would to dye clothes or fabric. It is lasting and changes what is immersed forever. He says it *saves us*—not the physical act of immersion to remove dirt, but rather something far more, a commandment of Jesus that is our "response to God from a clean conscience" and starts a new life. Because of these different uses and words for immersion in Hebrew, John the Baptist was careful to distinguish the purpose of the baptism he was performing as well as what was about to come with the Messiah, or Christ. "And so John the Baptist appeared in the wilderness, preaching a baptism of repentance for the forgiveness of sins" (Mark 1:4) John was baptizing "for the forgiveness of sins"; it wasn't just an outward sign. No one was claiming or even thinking they would receive forgiveness of sin without or before immersion; if so, what would be the point? The only requirement was to repent and humble yourself, something some people then and even today have a hard time doing, especially if they have become a leader.

Jesus humbled himself and was baptized, and it was then that the Spirit of GOD descended upon him. If John's baptism forgave sins, how much more important is baptism into the Christ that imparts the greatest gift of all, the "gift of the Holy Spirit?" (Acts 2:38) Understand that Scripture demonstrates different ways people received different measures of the Holy Spirit. John stated that the baptism of Jesus was more powerful than his, to the same extent that Jesus was more powerful and greater than he was. Not only does it forgive sins, as John's did, but it also imparts the Spirit of GOD into our lives as we are born again. "And this was his message: "After me comes the one more powerful than I, the straps of whose sandals I am not worthy to stoop down and untie. I baptize you with water, but he will baptize you with the Holy Spirit." (Mark 1:7-8) Anything less than forgiveness of sin and imparting the gift of the Holy Spirit, (Acts 2:38) would make the baptism of John the same as or even of less importance than the baptism into Jesus! So yes...I believe John, Jesus, Peter, and later Paul, all meant exactly what they said, and so should you. Jesus was very clear: the only way anybody can enter the "Kingdom of God" is to be born again, born of **both** water and spirit. However, it doesn't matter what I think, what you've been taught, what you've heard, or what you believe. The only thing that matters is what GOD thinks, what Jesus taught, and what the Spirit says. It's not my place to say who's saved, nor is it yours. Our only job is to surrender ourselves to God, and follow his words.

Having the kind of belief that causes faith is where we begin our journey, not end it. Have you seen, or do you remember, being in love as a teenager? We would do just about anything to be around, and look good to the one who we were infatuated with and had fallen for. Love causes action. That's the kind of love we need to have for Jesus, the kind of love in our heart that forms a deep faith in him. Love that causes us to do whatever he asks and the faith to speak it out loud. "If you confess with your mouth Jesus as Lord, and believe in your heart that God raised Him from the dead, you will be saved; for with the heart a person believes, resulting in righteousness, and with the mouth he confesses, resulting in salvation" (Rom 10:9-10 NASU) Declarations of conviction spoken out loud carry power. Just like the action of baptism, both confession and baptism are physical actions, ***not*** as works, and **never to "*earn*" anything**; that's impossible. What they are is simply part of the whole. They are what Jesus asks of us, the changing of the heart and the answer of our heart to GOD. They do not contradict each other, rather they supplement each other. Two different sides of the same coin, bound to each other and completely inseparable if you are to be born into his kingdom and become part of the family of GOD. "In Christ you are all children of God through faith for all of you who were baptized into Christ have clothed[5] yourselves with Christ." (Gal 3:26-27) Notice that we are clothed with Christ not when we believe, or pray, or even confess Christ, but when we are baptized. If you can let go of your pride and what people say, it's really

---

[5] Clothed #1746 enduo (en-doo'-o) (in the sense of sinking into a garment); to invest with clothing (literally or figuratively):

very simple; first coming to a place of faith and then being baptized into Christ is how we put on Christ, and when we put on Christ, we become **in** Christ. (Rom. 8:1)

The apostle Paul, writing to the young preacher Titus, brings it all together this way. Listen closely: "He saved us, not because of righteous things we had done, but because of his mercy. He saved us through the washing of rebirth and renewal by the Holy Spirit, whom he poured out on us generously through Jesus Christ our Savior, so that, having been justified by his grace, we might become heirs having the hope of eternal life." (Titus 3:5-7) How could it be more clear? It doesn't matter how bad you were or how good you are. We become chosen by GOD no longer by birth, but by choice. A rebirth through the water of baptism into Jesus Christ. It is then that by his grace we are renewed in spirit by receiving his Spirit and become heirs to an eternal life.

You can't change a recipe and expect to get the same results. When I was a teenager a friend and I were tasked with delivering a recipe for some kind of zucchini dish from his mom to mine. Being the teenager I was, and not wild about zucchini, I couldn't help playing with the recipe a little bit. A 3 became an 8, a 1 became a 7—you get the idea. What came out of the oven was nothing like the original. My mom couldn't figure it out until a phone call was placed to my friends mom, the one who gave it. The recipe was immediately changed back to the original and I had to eat the first one. It seems my mom also had a sense of humor. Changing a recipe on my mom was at least a little bit funny; changing Gods recipe for salvation to people hungering for God is not. You better believe that people who do so will be in a lot more trouble than I was and unless they make the proper changes, they will be forced to eat what they created, and will never taste the original.

It was less than fifty days after Jesus left the earth that the Holy Spirit descended upon the apostles and afterward Peter went out and preached the first sermon that started the church.[6] When those that first heard the Gospel, or good news, realized they were responsible for the death of the Christ, and were not right with GOD, "They were cut to the heart', and they cried out,'Brothers, what shall we do?' Peter replied,'Repent and be baptized, every one of you, in the name of Jesus Christ for the forgiveness of your sins. And you will receive the gift[7] of the Holy Spirit. The promise is for you and your children and for all who are far off—for all whom the Lord our God will call'.... Those who accepted his message were baptized, and about three thousand were added to their number that day." (Acts 2:37-41)

These words and instructions were not just a one-time thing for those responsible for the death of Jesus, or just the Jewish nation, but "for all who are far off"—that includes me, and it includes *you*. It has not changed, nor will it; doing the same thing that saved them and gave them the gift of the Holy Spirit will put us in a right relationship with GOD. It will not only save you and me, but it will also give us the gift

---

[6] Church #1577 ekklesia (ek-klay-see'-ah); a calling out,

[7] Gift #1431 dorea (do-reh-ah'); a gratuity: from #:1435; doron (do'-ron); a present; specially, a sacrifice:

of the Holy Spirit. If you have never come to God before, it's there for you. If you have believed, repented, and had a change of heart but have never been baptized "for the forgiveness of your sins" and "clothed yourself with Christ," I implore you to complete what you have begun. If you were sprinkled, or even immersed, being baptized but not for the forgiveness of your sins, or without belief, perhaps as a child, or for some other reason and not because you experienced a change of heart, I implore you to make it personal rather than just a ceremony, ritual, or christening. The baptism Jesus and the Bible teach is one-on-one between you and your Creator. No matter where we are at in our lives, and no matter our background, we all need to do it GOD's way. There are seven examples in the bible of people being saved,[8] and it's the same *every, single, time*. It's the way it works. It's an amazing opportunity, and it's really just not that hard. So why not? What are you waiting for??

"And now what are you waiting for? Get up, be baptized and wash[9] your sins away, calling on his name." (Acts 22:16) When you're ready, don't let anyone or anything stop you.

It seemed to me that was a great place to end the chapter, and that was my plan. However, while editing something else was

---

[8] Examples of people being saved; Acts 2:37-41, 8:5-13, 8:35-39, 10:34-48, 16:13-15, 16:31-34, and 22:10-18

[9] Wash #628 apolouo (ap-ol-oo'-o); to wash fully, i.e. (figuratively) have remitted (reflexively):

put on my heart one morning when I awoke, and I realized that there was another way to put it. I hope you enjoy.

There is a firm that is in charge of the unseen realm. They are far above anything on this earth in power, wealth, and majesty—so much so that they have no need of money or things of this world. Houses, cars, colored strips of paper, or shiny rocks—what we think of as important mean very little to them. They were there from the beginning and are everlasting. The chief executive officer is called YHWH or GOD he created everything and is in charge of everything on earth as well as the realm above. He made his son the chief financial officer, Yeshua Ha-Mashiach, or Jesus the Christ. The chief operating officer is called Ruach Ha-Kodesh (Roo-akh hak-koh-desh) or the Holy Spirit. The CEO hated the debts people were running up, so the CEO sent his son with a plan that would allow everybody to obtain a membership in the realm above. It was at that time he made him the CFO to make a way for our debts to be taken care of—a grace period, if you will. When the CFO left us he issued a credit card called Grace International. Those that became members received the card along with a hot line direct to the CEO. Any member could now operate under the grace period and have their debts taken care of just by calling[10] in and talking to the CEO. Just by keeping in touch, admitting your mistakes, and asking for the debts to be forgiven, the CFO would cover it! The COO would work with us to provide us

---

[10] If we confess our sins, he is faithful and just and will forgive us our sins and purify us from all unrighteousness. 1 John 1:9

with what we need, give us instructions to guide us, and show us how to live wisely. Show us how we can experience the joy that comes with keeping our debts low so that one day when we are called to the realm above, the books are opened, and your spreadsheet is reviewed by the CEO, the CFO will ever so gracefully declare that you are a member in good standing. You are part of the family, and your debts have been paid by Grace International. You show a zero balance and may now enter into the realm above, a place he has prepared for the debt-free.

That's what Grace International can do. Becoming a member is easy, as the conditions under the contract were made simple. The card is free; there are no annual, hidden, or even late fees. Anyone who is willing to admit their failures and humble themselves, can start afresh and be renewed as debt-free. The CFO is the only one who can issue a card with your name on it; there is no other way to get one or to receive the grace period. Without it, your debts will just keep piling up and accruing interest. So... what are you waiting for? Get up, call in, toss the fake paper one that came in the mail, and ask for your card. Then immediately[11] become a member[12] and activate it by following the rules the CFO laid out in the contract, or New Covenant. Read and follow the instructions the COO gave you. Stop pretending your debt doesn't exist, come clean, have all of your debt completely washed away, and start a new life with a membership in the realm above!

---

[11] Then immediately he and all his family were baptized. Acts 16:33
[12] Those who accepted his message were baptized, and about three thousand were added to their number that day. Acts 2:41

Chapter Five

The Way to Transformation

I mmediately after Jesus was baptized he was tempted by the devil, so don't be surprised if it happens to you too. You have made Satan very upset: he just lost something very valuable— *you*. He would love to get you back right away before you have time to grow in strength and become the person you are meant to be. While it's true that the devil is powerful and knows your weaknesses because of the time he spent around you, don't be afraid. Remember that when you were baptized you were "clothed" in Jesus, (Gal 3:27) and also that the Almighty has your back. "And God is faithful; he will not let you be tempted beyond what you can bear. But when you are tempted, he will also provide a way out so that you can endure it." (1 Cor 10:13) When you are at your weakest always remember that GOD is there with you. Always look for a way out; when you find it, you find GOD. When you take it, you are taking GOD into your life. Take comfort that GOD himself will come to your rescue and open doors for you. The only way the devil can hurt you is to get you back into your old way of thinking. That is why we must be completely transformed. "Do not conform to the pattern of this world, but be transformed by the renewing of your mind. Then you will be able to test and approve what God's will is—his good, pleasing and perfect will." Rom (12:2) It's time to look at things differently, to think differently, to act differently. It's time that we use a different standard for the way we test the things that we decide to let into our life. It's time to reject the way we once looked at things and reject anything that is patterned of this world. It's time to be transformed.

Transformed #3339 metamorphoo (met-am-or-fo'-o); to transform (literally or figuratively, "metamorphose"):

Ask any pilot—they all know what it means to make a go/no-go decision. It has to be done before every flight. The decision is made based on the weather that may be encountered, the condition of the airplane, and the condition of the pilot. Sometimes it's easy and sometimes it's hard. Every pilot has "personal minimums." Often-times it may be legal to make the flight, but still deemed unsafe based on the standard the pilot has set. And so it is in our walk with GOD. If we have been born again and have the Spirit living in us now we have to have a different standard than others and they are set individually. Having a beer or glass of wine is legal under God's law and may be no big deal for many, but not so for everybody. There may be people others can hang around with and minister to who would be unsafe for you to be around right now. While it's true that GOD is everywhere, we are not God, and there are some places we need to stay away from. Staying within your personal limits is very important for Christians as well as for pilots. Guaranteed every pilot has heard, often from their flight instructor, "There are old pilots and bold pilots but no old bold pilots."

Bad decisions always find a way to catch up with us. When writing to the church in Corinth about eating meat that had been sacrificed to idols, (1 Cor. 10:23) which was a controversial subject at that time, Paul says that just because something is lawful doesn't make it wise or constructive. A pilot with training and experience can expand their minimums to include flights that were unthinkable in the past and yet when any pilot pushes their envelope it can have fatal results. In our walk as Christians, it also takes training and knowledge as well as experience to avoid something that could be even worse. Training that comes from taking the time to read and study God's Word and experience that comes from putting it into action. A pilot will not improve without experience and training, making a commitment to change, and neither will we as Christians. If we are to live with Jesus in our hearts and be guided by the Holy Spirit it should go without saying change is required. Change in the things we say and do as well as the way we spend our time, and the way we think. Sometimes change is quick and purposeful, while other times it is gradual. When a pilot passes their check-ride they are immediately added to the Pilots Federal Database and receive the title of pilot. When we are born again, we are added to the Lamb's Book of Life (Rev. 21:27) and given the title of being his child. When we submit to doing it His way and truly put on Christ, it's a metamorphosis on a far greater scale than any accomplishment we could ever experience while we live. We become chosen by GOD and must undergo a complete transformation into a new life with Christ.

"I have been crucified with Christ and I no longer live, but Christ lives in me. The life I live in the body, I live by faith in the Son of God, who loved me and gave himself for me." (Gal 2:20) It's clear, over and over again, that the only way to start a new life is to first end the old.

"Put off your old self, which is being corrupted by its deceitful desires; to be made new in the attitude of your minds; and to put on the new self, created to be like God" (Eph 4:22-24) Bury your old life with it's goals and desires in the water of baptism and leave it there. Put on the new self, with a new attitude.

"Or don't you know that all of us who were baptized into Christ Jesus were baptized into his death? We were therefore buried with him through baptism into death in order that, just as Christ was raised from the dead through the glory of the Father, we too may live a new life." (Rom 6:3-4) Come out of the water like Christ came out of the tomb and live every day with him in your heart, guiding every step.

"No one can serve two masters. Either you will hate the one and love the other, or you will be devoted to the one and despise the other. You cannot serve both God and money" (Matt 6:24) "You can't reach for the stars with one hand in the mud."[1] If you want to be clean, perhaps you should stop playing in the mud. If you want to be spiritual then stop focusing on the physical. Learn to let go.

"Then Jesus said to his disciples, "Whoever wants to be my disciple must deny himself and take up their cross and follow me. For whoever wants to save his life will lose it, but whoever loses his life for me will find it. What good will it be for a someone to gain the whole world, yet forfeit their soul? Or what can anyone give in exchange for their soul?" (Matt 16:24-26)

I know people, and you probably do as well, who make the claim and call themselves Christians; but they have not put off their old life. They have not been born again, they have never been transformed, and they do not put God first. We all have a choice to make, and there are only two choices: our will or his. You can-not choose to agree with God 90 percent or even 99.9 percent of the time. His Word and his commands are absolute, whether we like it or not. If we are to be transformed we can never put our will above his. "For my thoughts are not your thoughts, neither are your ways my ways, "declares the Lord." (Isa 55:8) If you put your desires or beliefs over the Almighty GOD,

---

[1] Albert Lovelady

the timeless creator of life and every universe in the heavens, what does that say about you? Do you really think that's okay, that he's good with it? Maybe he'll say "Gee, I never thought of that"? This is no go to church once a week thing. Just being a "good" person isn't good enough. Being a member of a church or giving money won't do the trick; you're just wasting your time and money. There is no "fire insurance" here; no such thing as "one and done." "Jesus replied, "No one who puts a hand to the plow and looks back is fit for service in the kingdom of God." (Luke 9:62) Even Paul, the man GOD empowered and chose to write most of the New Testament said "I discipline my body and bring it into subjection, lest, when I have preached to others, I myself should become disqualified." (1 Cor 9:27) If any of that describes you, if you are not all in, listen up—you're missing out.

"Jesus replied, "Anyone who loves me, will obey my teaching. My Father will love them, and we will come to them and make our home with them." (John 14:23) Did you get that? We—no, **YOU**—have the opportunity to have the Creator of all things with you, in your spirit, your mind, and your very soul, walking with you, guiding you, listening to you, looking out for you every hour of every day! Not just some guardian angel but the one true living Almighty GOD and the Christ himself living with you, being guided by the Holy Spirit.[2] You don't have to involve another person to pray or call on, no one else needs to ask him to listen. He will hear **YOU**. Think

---

[2] The word for spirit was the same as wind or breath.

about how amazing that is—The Almighty, Creator of Heaven and Earth, promises to be as close to you as your own breath.[2] His only requirements here are once again the same two sides of the coin we see in all of his teachings; the changing of the heart: "love me" and the answer of our heart to GOD: "obey my teaching." Why would anyone want to miss out on that kind of relationship? What could be that important?

"Come to me, all you who are weary and burdened, and I will give you rest. Take my yoke upon you and learn from me, for I am gentle and humble in heart, and you will find rest for your souls. For my yoke is easy and my burden is light." (Matt 11:28-30) Notice he doesn't say he'll take all your burdens away, that all your problems, pain and sorrow will vanish in an instant, or that you're doing something wrong if problems, pain, and sadness come your way; in fact it's just the opposite! "Remember what I spoke to you: 'A servant is not greater than his master.' If they persecuted me, they will persecute you also." (John 15:20) What it does mean is that you don't have to carry the load yourself. When you are yoked with him, you can find rest and peace. He is not harsh, demanding, or unforgiving; rather, he is as gentle as he is powerful. He's been there, and he knows what it's like. Where you struggle to know the right thing to say and do, uncertain of tomorrow, he knows exactly what tomorrow holds; he knows the right words to use and the right thing to do. He knows the way, and he will teach you, if you are willing to learn, how to talk and just how to walk the walk. "But if anyone obeys his word, love for God is truly made complete in them. This is how we know we are in him: Whoever claims to live in him must walk as Jesus did." (I Jn 2:5-6) "*Must* walk as Jesus did." This is not an option or just a good idea. Heart and mind, thoughts and actions, one affecting the other day in and day out. Notice that obeying his word *completes*[3] GOD's love in you. When it comes to GOD's love, why would anyone not want to be complete?

"Present your bodies as a living sacrifice, holy and acceptable to God, which is your spiritual worship. Do not be conformed to this world, but be transformed by the renewal of your mind, that by testing you may discern what is the will of God, what is good and acceptable and perfect" (Rom 12:1-2 ESV) Too often we get it backward: it's not what GOD can do for you, as if he's a magic genie who fills our requests; it's about what he has already done for us. Too many times we become like spoiled children who get mad and stomp our feet when things don't go our way, when life gets hard and painful. Rather than look beyond the present and trust him, we cry out that he doesn't love us anymore. Did you catch what he is saying? When we surrender our life, our physical bodies, that becomes an act of spiritual worship. We see two sides of the coin once again, physical and spiritual tied together. When we first start our walk with the Father we experience the changing of the heart and the answer of our heart to GOD. As we age and transform there are times

---

[3] Complete; #5048 teleioo- to make perfect, to complete; to carry through completely, to accomplish, to finish, to bring to an end...to add what is yet wanting in order to render a thing full...

when our spirit follows the mind we have trained. Because of our knowledge and experience, we do what is right, not because our spirit is strong and we want to, but because we know it is the right way to think and act. It slowly becomes who we are, and that is spiritual worship. Even during times when our spirit is weak we do what is right because we know it pleases GOD.

If we are no longer conformed to the world, we no longer think and do the same things. We also no longer have the same worries and fears that others do, many of the same ones we had lived with also. We can take comfort that "We know that in all things God works for the good of those who love him, who have been called according to his purpose." (Rom 8:28) What once caused us worry and fear is now placed in the hands of our Father, the Almighty. And how does this happen? It happens when we are transformed by *renewing* our spirit and mind. "That you put off, concerning your former conduct, the old man which grows corrupt according to the deceitful lusts, and be renewed in the spirit of your mind," (Eph 4:22-23 NKJV) When you are able do that, you have the key to living with the Holy Spirit within you. You can set aside your old life, begin to change not only the way you think, but also the way you act, then you can see clearly to test the things you see and run into every day. As an insect that awkwardly crawls around in bushes undergoes a transformation, wings grow and it takes flight, we set aside the garbage that others wallow in and live in his "good, pleasing, and perfect will." That's when we take flight. That's what it means to be transformed.

Chapter Six

The Way to Live

Not long before Jesus was arrested, the religious leaders sent out people to try and trap Jesus by asking him what was the greatest commandment. He didn't miss a beat. "Love the Lord your God with all your heart and with all your soul and with all your mind." This is the first and greatest commandment. And the second is like it: 'Love your neighbor as yourself.' All the Law and the Prophets hang on these two commandments." (Matt. 22:37-40) *All of it*—EVERYTHING, every law, every commandment, including every prophet, everything anyone sent from GOD, even Jesus himself, ever told anyone to do comes down to and "hangs" on these two things: the love of GOD and the love of others. "The commandments, "You shall not commit adultery," "You shall not murder," "You shall not steal," "You shall not covet," and whatever other command there may be, are summed up in this one command: "Love your neighbor as yourself." Love does no harm to its neighbor. Therefore love is the fulfillment of the law." (Rom 13: 9-10)

Under GOD's law, you always know the right thing to do, how to talk, and how to act. Simply act out of love, be brazen, and always let it show. That's it!! However this is not always easy; there are a lot of harsh, stupid, unlovable people out there. You've probably seen some—sometimes they're in the mirror. Treating the unlovable with love is not an easy task. The only way that I know to do it is by first putting GOD's love in your heart. "A new command I give you: Love one another. As I have loved you, so you must love one another. By this all everyone will know that you are my disciples,[1] if you love one another." (John 13:34-35) Jesus declares we **must** love one another. Not to reach another level, not to preach or even work for a church, but to just simply be one of his disciples! That's all of us who make a decision to follow Jesus. That includes everyone, and that's all the time. "But I tell you, love your enemies and pray for those who persecute you,...If you love those who love you, what reward will you get?" (Matt 5:44-46) So how do *you* look at others? What are you known for? Does love show in your words and actions?

"We love because he first loved us. Whoever claims to love God yet hates a brother or sister is a liar. For whoever

---

[1] Disciple #3101 mathetes (math-ay-tes'); a learner, i.e. pupil...

does not love their brother and sister, whom they have seen, cannot love God, whom they have not seen. And he has given us this command: Anyone who loves God must also love their brother and sister." (1 John 4:19-21 ESV) I have to admit, it has taken me years to get to a point where I believe that I may understand what the Spirit is saying here. It just seems easy to love God while disrespecting others. I have come to an understanding that loving others is a choice that we make. It's one that is difficult at times, but not impossible. Like most things it becomes easier with practice and time. I believe he is saying that if you can't make the choice to love others, people you are in contact with, or have a relationship with, especially someone who is trying to follow God, then how can we really love GOD who we don't see and can't interact with in the same way? We don't love someone because they deserve it; we make the choice to love others because GOD does—and let's face it, none of us deserve it. If we receive GOD's love when we know we don't deserve it, don't we have to let go, make a choice, and love others even when they don't deserve it? Especially when someone is a believer as well? "And so we know and rely on the love God has for us. God is love. Whoever lives in love lives in God, and God in them." (I Jn. 4:16)

But what is love? An emotion, a feeling, maybe affection, something more? What is the kind of love the Holy Spirit is talking about? *Webster's Dictionary* gives about fourteen different definitions. GOD doesn't leave it to choice. "Love is patient, love is kind. It does not envy, it does not boast, it is not proud.

It does not dishoner others, it is not self-seeking, it is not easily angered, it keeps no record of wrongs. Love does not delight in evil but rejoices with the truth. It always protects, always trusts, always hopes, always perseveres." (1 Cor 13:4-7) All of the teachings of Jesus and the Holy Spirit throughout the bible are grounded in love. They show us over and over again just how to put love in our hearts and into action. It's so logical, so easy to say, but yet so hard to do. Dwelling on your failures won't help. However, I do believe that being aware of your failures improves your chances of getting it right next time. You would think it would be easier to implement in our lives as every time you go to what seems like the extreme and go out on a limb to follow what Jesus teaches, it just seems to work out. And it really can be rather extreme.

Give to everyone: "But I tell you, do not resist an evil person. If anyone slaps you on the right cheek, turn to them the other cheek also. And if anyone wants to sue you and take your shirt, hand over your coat as well. If anyone forces you to go one mile, go with them two miles. Give to the one who asks you, and do not turn away from the one who wants to borrow from you." (Matt 5:39-42 ESV) Can you imagine when being confronted by some jerk who is being brazenly demanding, obnoxious and overbearing, then turn around and give them even more than they are asking for? Sound crazy? Why would **anyone** do more than required when forced to do something you shouldn't have to do in the first place! How about making eye contact and talking with someone who has dirty, matted hair, dressed in filthy rags, and smells of booze, and then of all the crazy things, opening your wallet and giving them YOUR hard-earned money?? Sounding a little extreme yet? Then hold on to your hat because there's even more.

Never pass judgment on others: "Do not judge, or you too will be judged. For in the same way you judge others, you will be judged, and with the measure you use, it will be measured to you." (Matt 7:1-2) **NEVER** look down on or judge anyone for the clothes they wear, the way they think or act, or even the things they have done, say or do. You have no idea what they have been through, but GOD does. What would your life look like if you had been through what they have? Understand that when you put people down and judge others you are exalting yourself into the place of GOD! Trust me, that's not a good idea for any of us. "Who are you to judge someone else's servant? To their own master, severants stand or fall. And they will stand, for the Lord is able to make them stand." (Rom 14:4) When you judge someone, you are condemning yourself.

Always forgive others: "Then Peter came to Him and said, "Lord, how often shall my brother sin against me, and I forgive him? Up to seven times?" Jesus said to him, "I do not say to you, up to seven times, but up to seventy times seven." (Matt 18:21-22 NKJV) Have you ever noticed that *give* is the biggest part of *forgive*? Forgiving is for-giving. You can not forgive without giving, nor can someone forgive you without giving. It sounds silly but I read and quoited these scriptures many times individually for years without really stopping to understand the way Jesus ties forgiving and giving together. "Forgive, and you will be forgiven. Give, and it will be given to you. A good measure, pressed down, shaken together and running over, will be poured into your lap. For with the measure you use, it will be measured to you." (Luke 6:37-38) These are not two separate subjects. Jesus makes it fore-give. Before we can receive everything from God that He would like us to have, we must forgive. Over the years many writers have understood and proclaimed that when the injured party can forgive, they are the ones that benefit the most from having a clear conscience and releasing the burdens that weigh our spirit down. I believe Jesus is taking it even a step further. I believe he is teaching us that while it's true there is a natural relief and freeing of the spirit that comes from forgiving someone, there are also blessings direct from GOD. Perhaps it's because we become more like him when we forgive, because his forgiveness is his biggest gift to mankind. "Be perfect, therefore, as your heavenly Father is perfect." (Matt 5:48) It sounds so simple, but let's face it, it's not an easy thing to do. In fact it can be very hard. When someone close to you betrays you, spreads lies about you that destroy relationships, leaves you hurting, belittles you to others, and cuts you down it makes you want to lash out, tell your side, and put them in their place. When we are wronged it is in our base nature to strike back. Getting back is glorified in our movies and society. Yet we all know Jesus has been there, and worse. For Jesus it brought about an extremely painful death, and yet he still held his tongue and forgave them. "When they came to the place called the Skull, they crucified him there, along with the criminals—one on his right, the other on his left. Jesus said, "Father, forgive them, for they do not know what they are doing." (Luke 23:33-34) This is our example and our strength.

But that's not all. What happens when the shoe is on the other foot? As if forgiving is not hard enough, there is another side of this coin as well. "Therefore, if you are offering your gift at the altar and there remember that your brother or sister has something against you, leave your gift there in front of the altar. First go and be reconciled to them; then come and offer your gift." (Matt 5:23-24) Make the first move. It doesn't matter whose fault it was, or what caused it. It's not up to them to come to you or to just get over it. Jesus is saying it falls on your shoulders to be reconciled and make things right, and until you do you won't be right with GOD. It's true that there are some people who will not listen or forgive however, that doesn't relieve you of trying your best. Sometimes it can be very hard to go to someone who is critical of you and has taken offense at something you've said or done. Believe me, I know how hard it is to put yourself in that position, but just listening can begin the healing. Even if they can't forgive now, don't let it go. Don't just say you tried and give up; give it time. Remember the importance to Jesus of reaching an understanding, because he expects all of us to live this way. "If it is possible, as far as it depends on you, live at peace with everyone." (Rom 12:18) I know all of this sounds extreme and pretty much impossible to do once, let alone all the time. But just imagine for a moment a world where people lived this way.

The Torah, or Old Law, was just that—a law. Reading Leviticus can be tough. How many people sit down and read their insurance policy just for fun? Has any legal document made the best-seller list? In general, a lot of people look at the Bible like a legal document. When you do that, it's easy to use it to judge and convict others, standing tall and taking pride in ourselves. How do you move past that? We need to understand that the teachings of Jesus are more complex and challenging than any legal document; when you make it that you sell it short. GOD does not need a complexity of words with exacting definitions to get his point across, and he doesn't need you to try to understand legalese and jargon. The reality is that life is far more complex than anything any legal document can ever cover. A legal document sets down a framework for a specific item or action in black and white, whereas life is full of curves, and colors that change every day. Jesus fulfilled[2] the Torah, making it the Old Law, and brought forth something that fits every day, every situation, something that isn't hard to read and master but rather a thing of beauty. He is not asking you to master a law book; instead what he is asking you to master is—a coloring book.

Every day is a brand-new page, with new lines, another focus, and different challenges. He supplies the page, and the lines, he

---

[2] "Do not think that I have come to abolish the Law or the Prophets; I have not come to abolish them but to fulfill them" Matt 5:17

even supplies the colors; we hold the brush and go to work. We do our best to get it right, the right color matching the right number, a firm stroke just where it needs to be but not going too far. At the end of the day, when we close our eyes in sleep, we hand it in to our Father. He takes it and carefully places it in a book with our name on it, and while we sleep he prepares a new one for tomorrow. Some pages are harder than others, some colors are used regularly, and some rarely, but all are from him. The one turned in by the two year-old in Christ looks different and is easy to distinguish from the fourteen year-old as much as the one from the fifty year-old experienced painter. Others look at a finished work and judge it by the precision of the brush stroke and the use of color, but a loving Father judges a painting by the effort and love that went into it. No matter the outcome, the Father places them all with the same care in their respected books and loves them all just the same. To him, they are all beautiful just exactly the way they are. Only we see the mistakes and bobbles and the incomplete parts; he loves every single page and only sees the perfection[3] of the work of his children as they try to follow in his footsteps.

Like *Spy vs. Spy*, some want to make it Faith vs Works. GOD doesn't. The Bible doesn't. "We live [or walk, KJV] by faith, not by sight." (2 Cor 5:7) Walking, whether it's uphill or down, under the right conditions can be enjoyable and yet still be hard work. The way we live, the things we do every day, are works

---

[3] "Be perfect, therefore, as your heavenly Father is perfect." Matt 5:48

to be done in faith, two sides of the same coin. We are told to make our decisions "by faith not by sight"—not what we see, want, or what we would normally do, but shaping our lives by what GOD wants us to do, to trust him even when it may be hard or have a cost that can be tough to swallow. Our actions, or works, show what lies in the heart. To claim faith without works is just that—a claim. "What good is it, my brothers, if someone says he has faith but does not have works? Can that faith save him? If a brother or sister is poorly clothed and lacking in daily food, and one of you says to them, "Go in peace, be warmed and filled," without giving them the things needed for the body, what good is that? So also faith by itself, if it does not have works, is dead....Show me your faith apart from your works, and I will show you my faith by my works. You believe that God is one; you do well. Even the demons believe—and shudder!…For as the body apart from the spirit is dead, so also faith apart from works is dead." (James 2:14-26 ESV)

GOD's law and desire for every one of us is both thought and action, not just external but internal, and not just physical but spiritual. Like two sides of a coin that can-not be separated Jesus taught, "You have heard that it was said to the people long ago, 'You shall not murder, and anyone who murders will be subject to judgment. 'But I tell you that anyone who is angry with a brother or sister will be subject to judgment." (Matt 5:21-22) and "You have heard that it was said, 'You shall commit adultery.' But I tell you that anyone who looks at a woman lustfully has already committed adultery with her in his heart." (Matt 5:27-28) One side of the coin is internal, belief, knowledge, and faith the other side is external, what we do, our actions or works. Stamped on both sides is surrender. It starts in the mind, and if allowed, slowly moves to the heart, and then spreads through our lives and very existence.

GOD is asking—no actually he is demanding—that you be the person you instinctively know in your heart you should be. The way you were as a child. Not only in your actions but also in your thoughts, both in the way you think and treat others, as well as yourself. You can be at peace and change your whole world as well as the world of those around you just by knowing GOD's Word and then taking control and changing what you think on. "Finally, brothers and sisters, whatever is true, whatever is noble, whatever is right, whatever is pure, whatever is lovely, whatever is admirable—if anything is excellent or praiseworthy—think about such things. Whatever you have learned or received or heard from me, or seen in me—put it into practice. And the God of peace will be with you." (Phil 4:8-9) Put GOD in your mind, your heart, and your actions. His three-step plan for happiness and success.

I have heard people say "We live in a lost and dying world." While it's obvious that we are killing ourselves with pollution and trash, and that most people either don't believe, or will claim the name of Christ, but don't act like it; it still sounds terrible. We live an absolutely beautiful creation made by a powerful and loving God and we don't appreciate either enough. We only have a few short years that go by quickly to enjoy what we have been given and to do something with the time we have. Once we have discovered The Way and the joy of living with GOD, Jesus, and the Spirit within us, we have an obligation to share it; we have a job to do. "Then Jesus came to them and said, "All authority in heaven and on earth has been given to me. Therefore go and make disciples of all nations, baptizing them in the name of the Father and of the Son and of the Holy Spirit, and teaching them to obey everything I have commanded you. And surely I am with you always, to the very end of the age." (Matt 28:18-20) Living with the Spirit within us gives us happiness and joy, having knowledge of the Word gives us comfort and peace. Reaching heaven is our goal; giving this to others is our purpose.

"Neither do people light a lamp and put it under a bowl... In the same way, let your light shine before others, that they may see your good deeds and glorify your Father in heaven." (Matt 5:15-16) There's an old saying, "I would rather see a sermon than hear one anytime." The most powerful influence you can have for Jesus in this world is when you put love into action. It's true that no one really cares what you know until they know that you care. Once that happens, "Always be prepared to give an answer to everyone who asks you to give the reason for the hope that you have. But do this with gentleness and respect" (1 Peter 3:15)

I remember learning to snow ski on what's referred to as the bunny slope at the base of the mountain. While you are struggling to keep your balance and falling every ten to fifteen feet looking more like a wounded duck than a bunny, you're watching these people coming down the mountain, bouncing over bumps with incredible speed and confidence, and wondering how in the world do they do it! To make matters worse they are riding the chair lift right above you on the way to the top looking down on you. All the time no doubt laughing and making jokes. It wasn't until a few years later when I was on that chair to the top looking down that I realized that they weren't laughing. Every single one of them had been right where I had started as well. All I wanted to do now was to encourage them, to give them hope to hang in there and keep learning. It's going to take time, and there will be a few falls along the way, but it's worth the struggle to get to the top of the mountain. And so it is with our walk in the Spirit. If you have a hope in Jesus, there is a reason, you *always* need be ready to share it. We all know that when we're struggling few things help as much as encouragement from someone who's been there. If you're argumentative and don't show respect to others, you're not nearly as good as you think you are. You're not on your way to the top, and you're not changing anyone's mind, at least not in a positive way. With that kind of attitude, you're out of control, going downhill fast, and headed for disaster. Have you ever seen an athlete argue, yell, and scream at a referee, and then heard the referee say "Okay, when you put it that way I'll change the call"? Without gentleness and respect, you are just pushing people away, and just like the call, nothing changes.

We are to be around people who do things, and who have done things, that we may find repulsive and yet see the person separate from the sin. When people were looking down on a woman who had crashed a dinner party and sat in tears at Jesus' feet, he told them "Her sins, which are many, have been forgiven, for she loved much; but he who is forgiven little, loves little." (Luke 7:47 NASB) You never know the potential of the people who come into your life or just who GOD has sent, either to help you or for you to help. There are people you can reach that others can't. Who you share the Gospel with matters, even if you don't see the results. "I planted the seed, Apollos watered it, but God has been making it grow." (1 Cor 3:6-7) You never know how long it may take for a seed to grow; that's GOD's job. Sowing and watering the seed is ours. We need to be doing what we can to make the conditions right for growth, by loving and helping others. Not to be soil inspectors or seed counters; but rather to carry it with us and throw it out everywhere we go. To live and speak the truth as light in the darkness. "You are the light of the world...let your light shine before others, so that they may see your good works and give glory to your Father who is in heaven." (Matt. 5 14-16 ESV)

I had the privilege of "hangar flying" with some World War II fighter pilots. When I was lucky enough to be there, I was always mindful to stay in formation. For me, that consisted of sitting in an old hangar that had a slight whiff of AV gas and oil that was dripping from a radial engine from another era, on an old comfy chair that had been discarded some time ago, speak very little, and just listen to their war stories. One thing that stuck with me is that whenever they would find themselves out numbered, rather than be fearful and back off, they would call it a "target-rich environment." We also find ourselves in a target-rich environment. There are very few that fly the colors for all to see today. So usually we just try to stay out of the way and avoid contact, worried about getting shot down. They practiced, were prepared, and successful. You can be heaven's hero and do the same. "I tell you, there is rejoicing in the presence of the angels of God over one sinner who repents." (Lk 15:10) If you haven't done so, or it's been a while, it's time for a little target practice. You may need to do some maneuvering first, but take a few shots and see if anything hits, and you are able to start a conversion. If someone is in a rough spot, offer to pray for or with them, you may be surprised by their reaction. If by some chance you get shot down, don't worry; if it's too bad you can always bail out and find a new target. Talk to others in the squadron about how to improve, take it to the commander, but get back in, strap down, and stay in the fight. See if you can make the angels rejoice.

When you think of a great man or woman of God; who do you think of? You might think of someone with a title, someone who has a powerful position, or who is well-known. Maybe someone ordained who gets paid to preach every Sunday, could be a TV evangelist with a large following. Perhaps a successful author who has sold a lot of books, or a respected professor at a Bible college. GOD looks at things a little differently: "Whoever then humbles himself as this child, he is the greatest in the kingdom of heaven." (Matt 18:4 NASU) and "The greatest among you will be your servant. For whoever exalts himself will be humbled, and whoever humbles himself will be exalted." (Matt 23:11-12) To be great in people's eyes you need a sharp mind and a degree or some skill set others don't have, and then put in a lot of time, study, and practice. But that kind of greatness is temporary. To be great in GOD's eyes, now and in heaven, forever, you don't need any of that stuff!!! Just love people as they are, humble yourself, serve others, and in doing so spread the gospel! Pretty cool, right? "Do nothing out of selfish ambition or vain conceit. Rather in humility value others above yourselves, not looking to your own interests, but each of you to the interests of the others." (Phil 2:3-4)

Chapter Seven

The Way to Grow

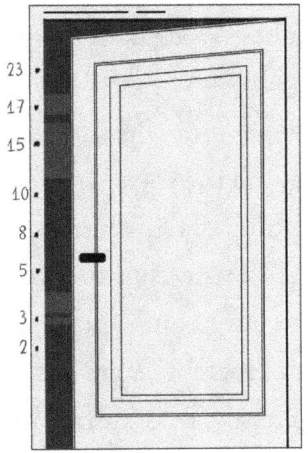

"Then we will no longer be infants, tossed back and forth by the waves, and blown here and there by every wind of teaching and by the cunning and craftiness of people in their deceitful scheming. Instead, speaking the truth in love, we will grow to become in every respect the mature body of him who is the Head, that is, Christ." (Eph 4:14-15) "Speaking the truth in love, we will grow." Truth without love is useless and cold, and love without truth is misguided and misses the mark. Two sides of the same coin. Even if one side is shiny and new, if the other side is tarnished and illegible, it can become worthless. Without growing in a balance of both, we are open to being deceived. We pretty much all mark and keep track of the growth of our children. Some of us, myself included, still have an unpainted section of a wall where their growth through the years, like memories, still exist. We're happy when they are growing tall and strong, and we get worried when they're not growing as they should. What makes you think God doesn't do the same with his children?

It is truly astonishing to me that no two snowflakes are the same. Think about it—all the snow that falls from the sky, and yet each snowflake is unique. Different surroundings and pressures make each one different. And so it is with people as well. Of all the people who have come and gone, you are different from every single one of them. You are truly unique and special. We all see things differently, react differently, and think differently. We have different abilities, talents, even shortcomings and temptations, and we all grow in different ways on different days. Like the snowflake we have all had different surroundings and pressures put on us that have shaped us and made each of us unique. Some find it easier to follow the heart and some find it easier to rely on the intellect. Look at what the Spirit is telling us. In order to be grounded and not be deceived by the scheming of the crafty and cunning who are on TV, radio, print, and social media, basically all around us, hitting us from all sides. And instead "grow up" in Christ, making him the head, the one in charge, you must be speaking the **truth** and doing it in **love**. Truth that comes from the intellect and knowledge of the Word. Love that comes from the heart and our emotions. Two sides of the same coin that are equally important for each one of us. Love grounded in truth, truth guided by love.

"This is love for God: to keep his commands. And his commands are not burdensome" (1 John 5:3) There are many who claim to love Jesus and to have the Spirit but do not see a reason to know his Word. We want his love, protection, and guidance—in effect the Spirit of GOD without any commandments, anything that might make us uncomfortable or contradict our well-established beliefs. But Jesus said, "If you love me, you will keep my commandments." (John 14:15 ESV) Why did Jesus say this? This is logical and not controversial in any way. If you love Jesus, you will keep his commandments, whatever they are. It should also be a little obvious that you can't do that without knowing what His commandments are. He continues on, "And I will ask the Father, and he will give you another Helper, to be with you forever...the Spirit of truth." (John 14:16-17 ESV) You can-not separate truth from the Spirit, nor can you have the Spirit of GOD without his Word. The only way to truly know GOD is through his Word because it is what brings us into a relationship with GOD, or as Jesus says, sanctifies us. Jesus asked GOD to "Sanctify[1] them by the truth; your word is truth." (John 17:17) If we are to know GOD, and be sanctified by him, we **have** to know his

---

[1] Sanctify #37 hagiazo (hag-ee-ad'-zo); to make holy, i.e. (ceremonially) purify or consecrate; (mentally) to venerate:

Word. We can't do it our way no matter how badly we want it to be true nor how logical or right it seems, it only leads to death. "There is a way that appears to be right, but in the end it leads to death." (Prov 14:12)

It is the Word that gives guidance, knowledge, and sanctification, for it is the product of the Spirit. Without GOD's Word in your heart, how do you know if you are following your own path, what seems right to you, rather than what is from GOD? Your thoughts or feelings, no matter how logical or well-intended or where they came from, will lead you to death and destruction. Knowing the Word of GOD is the only way to abide in him. "As the Father has loved me, so have I loved you. Now remain in my love. If you keep my commands, you will remain in my love, just as I have kept my Father's commands and remain in his love." (John 15:9-10) There is just no way around it; knowing what he commands and following through is how you know and show your love is real. And it's really not hard or painful; in fact, it can even become addictive.

"Like newborn babies, crave pure spiritual milk, so that by it you may grow up in your salvation," (1 Peter 2:2) Have you ever been around a hungry baby? That's the way we should look at God's Word. If we can't look back and see growth, we need to change our diet. The best way to learn God's Word is simply to read it. Look at the outline of the New Testament in the back of this book, pick one and spend fifteen or twenty minutes reading it. That's it; it's not hard. Sermons, classes, books, and seminars can give enlightenment or be boring. Even worse they can be wrong, misleading, or deceitful. On the other hand, reading the words of Jesus and the Spirit rarely disappoint and are always true. "Let the word of Christ dwell in you richly, teaching and admonishing one another in all wisdom."(Col 3:16 ESV) The joy of reading God's Word is like the joy of eating a nice big layered cake—it looks whole but once you cut into it and the more you taste it, the more you start to see the different layers and taste the flavors. "And this is my prayer: that your love may abound more and more in knowledge and depth of insight, so that you may be able to discern what is best and may be pure and blameless" (Phil 1:9-10) Without knowledge, love has no direction or depth, no insight, and no discernment. When love abounds in knowledge one becomes pure and blameless before GOD. A **GREAT** place to be.

I know people who know the truth well, rely on it, and stop there. It seems they are always looking to increase in knowledge as the goal rather than embracing and growing in the Spirit as well. There are those that take pride in knowledge and preaching to others without noticing the log stuck in their own eye.[2] Instead of just trying to rely on our knowledge and our search for perfection in it, we need to also be nurturing and growing in the Spirit. "And if anyone does not have the Spirit of Christ, they do not belong to Christ." (Rom 8:9) Without the spirit of love in our hearts, we are nothing. "If I

---

[2] "Why do you look at the speck that is in your brother's eye, but do not notice the log that is in your own eye?" Matt 7:3 NASU

speak in the tongues of men and of angels, but have not love, I am a noisy gong or a clanging cymbal. And if I have prophetic powers, and understand all mysteries and all knowledge, and if I have all faith, so as to remove mountains, but have not love, I am nothing. If I give away all I have, and if I deliver up my body to be burned, but have not love, I gain nothing." (1 Cor 13:1-3 ESV)

The problem is that no one who has studied and knows the truth would ever think that they don't have the Spirit. But actions speak louder than words and show the true heart. The Word of God needs to reside not just in the mind and intellect but also in the heart so that it shows in our actions as well. You can tell what kind of a tree it is by looking at its fruit.[3] If the spirit of GOD is love, is it showing in your day-to-day actions? Have you found yourself being critical of anyone lately, or agreeing with others when they are? Perhaps someone affiliated with a different political party? Perhaps some sinner who has a different belief, someone from some other group or church? When someone in dirty clothes on the corner, or walking by your car, asks for money, are you happy to give, or do you make an excuse, rationalize, or look down on them? When someone is dressed differently, perhaps inappropriately, or maybe dressed up as a person of the opposite sex, are you able to reach out with compassion and love, or are you critical, harsh, and ready

---

[3] "By their fruit you will recognize them. Do people pick grapes from thorn-bushes, or figs from thistles? Matt 7:16-17

to condemn? Do immigrants, or people of another ethnic group who are asking for a "free handout" or undeserved help bother you, or do you treat them with love, giving beyond exception? Have you ever allowed someone in your home who needed help, would you? How about the young single mother living in fear and poverty, forced to become hard and tough to survive, or the pregnant girl who is barely a teenager? If you believe she should have the child what help do you offer her? How about the addicted, the alcoholic, the prostitute with an STD, someone doing porn, the gang member, or the thief? Then there's the police officer who made a mistake, or who has become hardened by the job and what they face; do you feel love for them or anger? After all, they all knew what they were getting into; do they get what they deserve? Are these the kind of people you embrace, or avoid? You might as well be honest with yourself, GOD already knows. Perhaps you are someone that somewhere in all of that the description came a little close to home and was easy for you to relate to. Maybe that's where you've been or it's the direction you might be headed. If you can relate, take comfort, because that makes you the kind of person Jesus spent his time with, forgave, healed, had mercy on, and loved. And guess what—he still does today. Suppose you learned that Jesus was down by the mission, sitting in the filth with the alcoholics, tweakers, and prostitutes; would that surprise you? Would you drop everything and head down to sit with him? Would it make you uncomfortable? Might you pause a little, worried about what others might think of you?

"If you love those who love you, what credit is that to you? Even sinners love those who love them. And if you do good to those who are good to you, what credit is that to you? Even sinners do that. And if you lend to those from whom you expect repayment, what credit is that to you? Even sinners lend to sinners, expecting to be repaid in full. But love your enemies, do good to them, and lend to them without expecting to get anything back. Then your reward will be great, and you will be children of the Most High, because he is kind to the ungrateful and wicked. Be merciful, just as your Father is merciful." (Luke 6:32-36) It sounds so simple to treat everybody with love; however, it's much harder to put into action. Do you remove the uncomfortable part by just staying with the people you are comfortable with? Take some time to truthfully examine yourself, and your attitudes. Jesus already has.

"I am the vine; you are the branches. If you remain in me and I in you, you will bear much fruit; apart from me you can do nothing. If you do not remain in me, you are like a branch that is thrown away and withers; such branches are picked up, thrown into the fire and burned. If you remain in me and my words remain in you, ask whatever you wish, and it will be done for you." (John 15:5-7) So how do you connect to, remain, and grow in Jesus? For many of us, it can be hard to connect to and love GOD the way we would like. Often he seems so far away and disconnected from our lives and the things we face day by day. We think, *What's wrong with us that we can't connect the way others seem to find it so easy to? Are they fools, is he really there or is it just me—does he not love me?* How do you feel his presence?

"Submit yourselves, then, to God. Resist the devil, and he will flee from you. Come near to God and he will come near to you." (James 4:7-8) This is not an idle statement—this is a promise. First of all, you will never come close to GOD until you look for, recognize, renounce, and actively resist the devil. But how do you move away from the comfort of the devil to the comfort of GOD? You start by removing that which is from Satan. Let go of all of the seemingly little things you are hanging on to. Pray out loud, and renounce Satan, specifically that which has a hold on you. There is power in words and they give strength to our actions. If you have never done it before, don't wait, do it now.

Then how do you come near to GOD? Ask a hundred people and you will get a hundred different answers. A lot of things can cause us to feel close to GOD, listening to music, being in nature, helping others, meditating, joining in a worship service, they are all great and wonderful. But what does GOD say, what does HE want us to do? "Let us draw near to God with a sincere heart and with the full assurance that faith brings, having our hearts sprinkled to cleanse us from a guilty conscience and having our bodies washed with pure water." (Heb 10:22-23) These two verses teach us to begin by sincerely and fully, submitting to GOD. If you can't sincerely submit fully to GOD, nothing will change. You will never grow close or draw near to Him. You must submit yourself with a full faith, and then you can have full assurance that he hears you. But there's more.

When we are baptized, water washes over our whole body. It is a death of the old life and the beginning of a new one. "Your old sin-loving nature was buried with him by baptism when he died; and when God the Father, with glorious power, brought him back to life again, you were given his wonderful new life to enjoy." (Rom 6:4 TLB) It is far more than just a physical action The Spirit tells us that he immerses us with "pure water." You can-not find this pure water anywhere around here, all water on earth has some kind of contaminant. The water he is talking about it is pure because it comes from above, removes sin, and starts a new life. The heart, on the other hand, does not need a death and rebirth; rather it needs a cleansing and a complete change. I was in Arizona during the heat of summer. When we got out of our nice air-conditioned car and headed across the smoldering parking lot toward the back patio of the restaurant, I noticed people sitting outside under an awning in the heat. How in the world can this be? I realize that I don't live here, but nobody could get used to this kind of heat! As we got closer I could feel it getting cooler and see the water misting the whole area. As we walked through the water it was incredibly refreshing and felt absolutely wonderful. That's what happens when our hearts are sprinkled. When the heart is sprinkled it is refreshed and changed (and it feels pretty wonderful). Having a change of heart to cleanse our guilty conscience and having our bodies washed in pure water is the way to draw near to

GOD. The changing of the heart and the answer of our heart to GOD will allow His Spirit to live and grow within us.

Things that are intangible can be scary and difficult to embrace however, "God is spirit" (John 4:24) and he created us with a spirit as well. "The Spirit himself testifies with our spirit that we are God's children." (Rom 8:16-17) You were made, and "hardwired" if you will, with a direct line to GOD, the Creator, and Master of the Universe, and he will hear you without an appointment, anytime, day or night. He's never too busy, and will never put you on hold. He is available right now, at this very minute for you, so how do you do it? "What am I to do? I will pray with my spirit, but I will pray with my mind[4] also" (1 Cor 14:15 ESV) I often don't know what to say, or say it the wrong way. It's only later, usually in the middle of the night, that it hits me what I should've said. But once the words are spoken, you can't back up and delete. Don't know what to say when you pray? Worse yet maybe say something dumb and sound foolish, or even offend GOD, saying something stupid that you will later regret? Guess what—you can't! "The Spirit helps us in our weakness. For we do not know what to pray for as we ought, but the Spirit himself intercedes for us with groanings too deep for words. And he who searches hearts knows what is the mind of the Spirit, because the Spirit intercedes for the saints according to the will of God." (Rom

---

[4] Mind #3563 nous (nooce); the intellect, i.e. mind (divine or human; in thought, feeling, or will)

8:26-27 RSV) He is your Father and Friend, he gave you your spirit, and he knows you well. "And when you pray, do not keep on babbling like pagans, for they think they will be heard because of their many words. Do not be like them, for your Father knows what you need before you ask him." (Matt 6:7-8) Prayer should be less about the words and more about opening the heart. Once you start to pray that way, the closer you come to GOD. A well-renowned Puritan named John Owen once said about prayer "Friendship is most maintained and kept up by visits; and these, the more free and less occasioned by urgent business." The only thing you can do wrong is to ignore him.

Growing closer to GOD takes time, effort, thought, and training. No one enters a marathon without training. No one wins a gold medal without training, as well as years of dedication, and perseverance. No one would dare step into a boxing ring against a powerful opponent without knowing what they were doing. "Do you not know that in a race all the runners compete, but only one receives the prize? So run that you may obtain it. Every athlete exercises self-control in all things. They do it to receive a perishable wreath, but we an imperishable. So I do not run aimlessly; I do not box as one beating the air. But I discipline my body and keep it under control, lest after preaching to others I myself should be disqualified." (1 Cor 9:24-27 ESV) We are in the race for the long haul, and we are in it to win it. A successful training program is not an easy one. It often requires us to do things differently than we would on our own. A good workout can be exhausting while at the same time feel wonderful, and we all know the advantages that come with it. Just as physical exercise produces strength, the trials of life can do the same. "Consider it pure joy, my brothers and sisters, whenever you face trials of many kinds, because you know that the testing of your faith develops perseverance. Let perseverance finish its work so that you may be mature and complete, not lacking anything." (James 1:2-4) The more we grow, both in spirit and knowledge, the happier, more confident, and peaceful our lives become. Growing in faith doesn't mean becoming a stronger person; it's just the opposite—we become weaker because GOD is stronger in our life. The more we learn to rely upon and trust the Father rather than ourselves the less stress, worry, and fear we carry around and the more prepared we are when trials come our way.

Years ago I was in charge of communications at a rather large air show. Every year emergency services would have a round-table discussion where all involved would run through different scenarios. They were always kind of fun and it was not too important—until it was. One year, there was a plane crash. Immediately, I knew exactly what calls to make and what needed to be done without thinking, because without even realizing it, I was prepared. Thanks to the quick and proper response by everyone involved, the pilot made a full recovery. We don't need to be sheltered; we need to be prepared to stand face to face, toe to toe with the devil himself, and not back down. Notice the last part of this verse, "Submit yourselves, then, to God. Resist the devil, and he will flee from you." (James 4:7)

I'm sorry, but how cool is that? You don't run from the devil, he runs from you! But you must prepare. First you need to submit to GOD. Listen to your coach and trainer. We have a coach who has fought Satan himself, and won. Not only did he hold up under temptations and trials, but Jesus even overcame death. We also have a trainer who will guide us, "I will ask the Father, and he will give you another Advocate to be with you forever— the Spirit of truth...But the Advocate, the Holy Spirit, whom the Father will send in my name, will teach you all things and will remind you of everything I have said to you." (John 14:16-17, 26-27) We don't rely on the teachings of men to guide us. The Holy Spirit sent from GOD taught and reminded the writers of the New Testament of everything Jesus said and everything GOD wants us to know. And he's still here for you if you will only listen. We don't hear the Spirit of God when we are busy talking, and we can't follow when we are in the lead. Sometimes we just need to stop, look, and listen. Like the child who runs ahead, we need to turn around, listen, look up to our Father, and learn to wait on him, he knows and will guide us in The Way.

Which brings us to a request. I want to ask you to walk in The Way tomorrow. Start the day with a prayer and ask GOD for his help, to be close to you and guide you. Then, as you go about your day, doing whatever is planned or just comes up, while you're taking care of what needs to be done, treat everyone you have any contact with—with love. The people at work, the people in line, all of the people you interact with—every single person. Everyone from the clerk in the store to the people on the road. From the faceless person on the computer or phone to the faces you see all the time. No harsh words, no complaining; check the negative thoughts, words, and deeds for just one day. Instead of ignoring people, take the initiative and reach out with kindness, joy, respect, and love all day long. Even to those who don't expect it or deserve it. And for goodness sake don't exclude family and those you live with or see every day. Get out of the rut and break the mold with a little extra kindness and warmth for them; after all, they are putting up with you. If you are confronted with frustration or anger, respond with love just this one time. Watch your tone; how you speak can be just as important as what you say. Then end the day tomorrow with ten to twenty minutes of reading his Word, pray, and be open to wherever you are led.

Make an effort to try it just once and see how it works out. Don't be afraid to try. If you fail that's okay; you can always try again. See how it feels and how others respond. Then maybe you can try it twice a week or who knows? Maybe more. See if it doesn't bring a little more joy and happiness to you and those around you. Perhaps you might even find yourself being treated just a little bit better. You could even find yourself doing it without trying. See if by showing love to all you aren't just a little bit closer to heaven and growing a little bit closer to GOD himself.

Chapter Eight

The Way to Worship

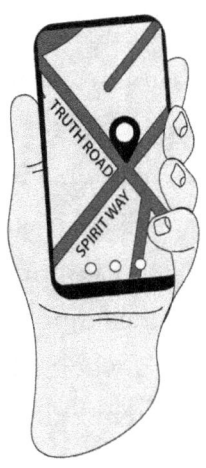

M any religions ask their followers to go on a pilgrimage or have their headquarters at a certain place where you can go to meet their leaders, or maybe go for a special worship or event. When asked where people should worship, Jesus responded, "Yet a time is coming and has now come when the true worshipers will worship the Father in the Spirit and truth, for they are the kind of worshipers the Father seeks. God is spirit, and his worshipers must worship in the Spirit and in truth." (John 4:23-24) At the time Jesus spoke these words GOD had asked the Jews to come to Jerusalem several times a year to remember events from the past. But not under the new covenant given by Jesus. I have searched the world with Google Maps, and as far as I can tell, Spirit Way and Truth Road never cross. However, when we input it into our internal GPS it will give us directions no matter where we are, or how far away. We may have gotten sidetracked on our journey so it may take a while to get there, but it's worth the trip. It doesn't matter which one you're closer to or if you arrive by Spirit or Truth; you haven't reached your destination until you find both, and arrive at the intersection where they come together.

Are you starting to notice a pattern here? Just as we were created both physical and with a spirit, both are required to be given to GOD in all we do, including worship. Jesus announces here that he is ushering in a whole new way of worship and that now GOD seeks a different kind of worshiper—one who worships in spirit and truth, with their heart and mind. Not at a certain place once or twice a year, or even weekly, but rather every day, all the time. Wherever we may be we can come close to, worship, and praise the Almighty. Because if there are no physical coordinates on a map for us, that means we must worship internally. That also means we don't have to mark it on our calendar or wait until everyone gets there; you can go ahead and start now.

Just understanding who GOD is—his power, wisdom, knowledge, understanding, and love—should put us in awe and cause us to worship him in spirit. When we begin to worship GOD in spirit everyday there is a lot less worry, stress, disappointment, and depression. Even sin and temptation begin to lose power over us. To worship GOD in truth, you have to know the truth, and no matter what anyone says it really does take a little bit of work. "Work out your salvation with fear and trembling" (Phil 2:12) Just belonging to, or joining a church won't do it. Nobody, regardless of education or title, can work out anybody else's salvation. Only you are responsible for you, and no one else. You really don't have to take anyone's word for it when you can look it up and read it yourself. There is a tremendous joy in knowing the Word of GOD better; it's how we stay grounded in our everyday life. "If indeed you continue in the faith, grounded and steadfast, and are not moved away from the hope of the gospel which you heard" (Col 1:23 NKJV) You and I have decisions to make, ones we should be knowledgeable about and not take lightly.

"These people honor me with their lips, but their hearts are far from me. They worship me in vain; their teachings are merely human rules." (Matt 15:8-9) Is Jesus really saying that people can set their alarm, get dressed up every Sunday, go to church, and it's all in vain, all for nothing? I know it might sound harsh, but it seems that way to me. It was true when Jesus said it, and it's still true today. Many religions have a group of people in a big building who send down edicts to congregations where men in fancy robes stand and preach every Sunday. In this ever-changing world, they decide who can be a member, what principles will be taught, what is a sin, and what is okay. The same thing is true with many of the TV evangelists and mega-churches and some smaller ones as well. Sometimes it's well intended and good. However, too often they make decisions that take into account how people will feel about it, does it fit society's view, will it gain or lose members, and will they give more or less, rather than what God says. For that–you can find out yourself. Not long after Jesus left the earth, and long before TV and mass media, it was already happening. We are warned, "See to it that no one takes you captive through hollow and deceptive philosophy, which depends on human tradition and the elemental spiritual forces of this world rather than on Christ. For in Christ all the fullness[1] of the Deity lives in bodily form, and in Christ you have been brought to fullness. He is the head over every power and authority." (Col 2:8-10) There are a lot of deceptive philosophies that come from traditions and even the "elemental *spiritual forces* of this world." While they can sound good, make no mistake, all of them are hollow and will take you away from Christ.

None of us, not one, has the wisdom, knowledge, or intelligence to take the place of or speak for Jesus. It is he alone who received power and knowledge from on high. He is the only one to whom GOD has ever said, "As soon as Jesus was baptized, he went up out of the water. At that moment heaven was opened, and he saw the Spirit of God descending like a dove and alighting on him. And a voice from heaven said,

---

[1] Fullness # 4138 pleroma (play'-ro-mah); repletion or completion, i.e. (subjectively) what fills (as contents, supplement, copiousness, multitude), or (objectively) what is filled (as container, performance, period):

"This is my Son, whom I love; with him I am well pleased."
(Matt 3:16-17) And again later, "Then a cloud appeared and
covered them, and a voice came from the cloud: "This is my
Son, whom I love. Listen to him!" (Mark 9:7) When the Spirit,
in Colossians 2: 8-10, tells us that Christ has all the *fullness* of
the Deity, or GOD, in him and that we have been given *fullness*
in Jesus Christ that means, full to the brim, literally "completion" there is no room for anything from anyone else. Regarding
people becoming religious leaders, telling others what to do,
and taking titles Jesus was quite clear; "But you are not to be
called rabbi, for you have one teacher, and you are all brethren.
And call no man your father on earth, for you have one Father,
who is in heaven. Neither be called masters, for you have one
master, the Christ." (Matt 23:8-10 RSV) It is clear from the
context in which Jesus spoke that he is talking about people
taking a title, not forbidding the use of these words altogether.
I called my physical father my *father* because it described him,
and while he was a good example, preached the Gospel, led
worship services, and taught Bible classes, being a father and
even a teacher was a description of what he did, never a title.

Does this mean we no longer need to meet together in a
place of worship? Nope, not at all! "Let us hold unswervingly
to the hope we profess, for he who promised is faithful. And let
us consider how we may spur one another on toward love and
good deeds, not give up meeting together, as some are in the
habit of doing, but encouraging one another" (Heb 10:23-25)
And when were they meeting? "On the first day of the week

we came together to break bread. Paul spoke to the people"
(Acts 20:7) Coming together to praise and worship GOD, as
well as "break bread together," is part of what keeps us close
to GOD. Have you ever noticed the log that is removed from
the fire dies out much quicker than the ones that are together?
When we worship together not only does it lift GOD up, as if
that wasn't enough, but it lifts us up also, as well as others who
have decided to live their life in him. It is important that we
worship physically with our bodies as well as with our spirit.
"I appeal to you therefore, brothers, by the mercies of God, to
present your bodies as a living sacrifice, holy and acceptable to
God, which is your spiritual worship." (Rom 12:1 ESV) If we
are to worship GOD in spirit "which is your spiritual worship"
it has to show in our actions "present your bodies as a living
sacrifices." This is how we worship, this is how we please GOD.

There are hundreds of churches out there. With so many
choices how do you pick one? First of all, does size matter? Are
the people at the mega church any better off than the people at
the corner church?" There are obvious advantages and disadvan-
tages to large congregations as there are for small ones. Jesus says
it doesn't matter. "For where two or three gather in my name,
there am I with them." (Matt 18:20) Second thing, don't set
your exceptions too high. You will never find a church with a
group of perfect people. If you do, you will not be able to join,
because the minute you do you will ruin it.[2] Too many times

---

[2] From John Clayton; Does God Exist?

I have seen people jump from one church to another always complaining and not realizing where the real problem was. I have heard it said, "Wherever you go—there you are."[3] So how do you find people you can put up with? What do you look for? Is it just personal preference? Churches certainly are not all the same. Does GOD give us guidelines? Just how does he describe His church? Three things stand out.

First, it's natural to think it's all about what they are doing, and that's important; however, first and foremost, it's not what they do, it's how they act. "By this everyone will know that you are my disciples, if you love one another." (John 13:35) If you're with a group that as a whole does not love one another, as well as others, you are not with Christ's disciples. It doesn't matter if you have the same hobbies, see things the same way, belong to the same political party, or are of the same race or background. Love *has* to transcend all of that. If it doesn't, you're in the wrong place. I have seen churches split apart over the smallest of things because pride replaced love.

Second, whether it's a small group or a large one, leadership matters. I have seen it over and over again: nothing can hurt more people and do more harm faster than a church with unqualified leadership. "Where there is no vision, the people perish" (Prov 29:18 KJV) Without a rudder, a ship will wind up in ruin. Without direction in leadership and guidance, a church will do more harm than good. Often-times it happens

---

[3] From the video series; Discovering the Jewish Jesus.

over and over again. There will always arise disagreements, without the proper leadership arguments grow, people leave, and the church suffers. The Apostle Paul was starting churches all over the Mediterranean, constantly throughout his life and the leadership God had him put in place was consistent. "The reason I left you in Crete was that you might straighten out what was left unfinished and appoint elders in every town, as I directed you. An elder must be blameless, faithful to his wife, a man whose children believe and are not open to the charge of being wild and disobedient. Since an overseer manages God's household, he must be blameless — not overbearing, not quick-tempered, not given to drunkenness, not violent, not pursuing dishonest gain. Rather he must be hospitable, one who loves what is good, who is self-controlled, upright, holy and disciplined. He must hold firmly to the trustworthy message as it has been taught, so that he can encourage others by sound doctrine and refute those who oppose it." (Titus 1:5-9) In any group a leadership will arise, but in the church established by Jesus it should have the leadership that God put in place.

The third, and most important, is understanding the importance of God's Word. "And God said, "Let there be light," and there was light." (Gen 1:3) Whether it was actual vibrations or some other force we don't understand, there is more power in GOD's words than we can ever possibly fathom. Nothing else even comes close. You should have nothing to do with anyone or any group that is dismissive, takes lightly, changes any meaning, or in any way alters the Word of GOD. It was, and still is, the very essence of Jesus. "In the beginning was the Word, and the Word was with God, and the Word was God. He was with God in the beginning" (John 1:1-2) and "The Word became flesh and made his dwelling among us. We have seen his glory, the glory of the one and only Son, who came from the Father, full of grace and truth." (John 1:14) Gods grace flows through the truth in his Word. If we want to do God's will, we need to be around others who put Jesus first. People who are committed to following Him, as well as listening to, helping, and lifting each other up. Even a small, easy-to-break chip of wood, when glued to others, becomes a strong sheet of plywood.

Never listen to someone no matter how they present themselves, how well they speak, how smart or persuasive they are, if they are speaking on their own. "Jesus answered, "My teaching is not my own. It comes from the one who sent me. Anyone who chooses to do the will of God will, will find out whether my teaching comes from God or whether I speak on my own. Whoever speaks on their own does so to gain personal glory" (John 7:16-18) Later he said, "I and the Father are one." (John 10:30) Remember that back in 740 to 700 BC the prophet Isaiah wrote "This people honors me with their lips, but their heart is far from me; in vain do they worship me, teaching as doctrines the commandments of men." (Isa 29:13 ESV) Jesus quoted Isaiah and then added "You leave the commandment of God and hold to the tradition of men." (Mark 7:8 ESV) If a church is openly teaching rules or traditions of men, it's time to move on. Since for the most part all churches claim to follow and teach God's Word, as did the people Jesus was speaking to, it becomes all the more important to check and find a group where God's Word is not only taught but also held as the only standard by which decisions are made. It falls on you to make sure that what you are hearing, what you are believing, and what you are speaking is the truth. No one is perfect, and you should not expect anyone, even yourself, to be right or agree about everything. One of the biggest reasons to get together is to support and learn from one another. What you can expect, is for love to overcome pride. While who you worship, relax, and associate with is important, remember, you alone are responsible for you alone. Will there be hypocrites there? Probably. People who are judgmental and look down on others? It's likely. However, with a little luck there will also be others that are there to worship GOD, learn more, and celebrate walking in The Way, and not just in the good times but in every situation they face. They come in all shapes, sizes, ages, and colors. It doesn't matter their background, citizenship, or political party; those are the people you want to find, be around, and befriend. They are the ones who will lift you up, give you strength, and brighten your day. If your in a church that doesn't have a group like that—start one.

If you are leading or teaching, or if you are someone that others look to, you already know you have a greater responsibility. "My brethren, let not many of you become teachers, knowing that we shall receive a stricter judgment. For we all stumble in many things." (James 3:1-2 NKJV) Make sure you are not tempted with pride and that your opinions are always given as just that—an opinion and open to change. Always listen and never presume. There have been many times when I have found that the most uneducated and least experienced student, even someone I may have thought of as perhaps "a half a bubble off," will deliver the most profound observation, something I would never have thought of. That is why, "The one who receives instruction in the word should share all good things with their instructor." (Gal 6:6) and remember, "One is your Teacher, the Christ, and you are all brethren...And whoever exalts himself will be humbled, and he who humbles himself will be exalted." (Matt 23:8, 12 NKJV) Stay grounded in the Word, and GOD will bless you. GOD desires that all people worship Him in truth and for that to happen teachers are required. The backbone of every church are leaders and teachers who will stand for and are always ready to speak the truth. During the Last Supper, Jesus prayed "Sanctify them by the truth; your word is truth." (John 17:17) Blessed will be the hands that carry the torch and shine light.

Chapter Nine

The Way to Avoid

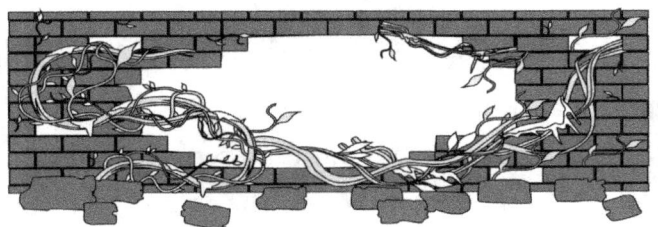

"Examine everything carefully; hold fast to that which is good; abstain from every form of evil." (1 Thess 5:21-22 NASU) It would be nice if the two sides of the coin were just to love GOD and to love your neighbor; however, love can be misplaced as well. We have all probably seen or experienced the pain and scars that can come when this happens. "People will be lovers of themselves, lovers of money, boastful, proud, abusive, disobedient to their parents, ungrateful, unholy, without love, unforgiving, slanderous, without self-control, brutal, not lovers of the good, treacherous, rash, conceited, lovers of pleasure rather than lovers of God—having a form of godliness but denying its power. Have nothing to do with such people." (2 Tim 3:2-5)

These people he is speaking of here are not portraying themselves as atheists; he says they have "a form of godliness but [deny] its power." They may appear to be, or claim to be, Christians; however, by living this way they do not have, or understand the type of power that comes with having Godliness in the heart. Some even see humility as a sign of weakness. It is very clear that all of the divisiveness, selflessness, disrespect of others, greed, boasting, and so on that we see today has absolutely **no** place in anyone's life who is following GOD. **Neither** is being with, listening to, agreeing, following, or supporting people who are!! He says to "have **nothing** to do with such people." We have a choice, and not everyone finds, or even looks for, The Way. "Enter through the narrow gate. For wide is the gate and broad is the road that leads to destruction, and many enter through it. But small is the gate and narrow the road that leads to life, and only a few find it." (Matt 7:13-14 ESV) For most people something always gets in the way of getting in The Way. You would think that this kind of behavior would be easy to spot and avoid; however, there seems to be something about this type of person or personality, that attracts too many otherwise good people. Like a good salesman they know how to appeal to a lot of people, and that kind of release can be very appealing, like a drug. They are selling instant gratification through pride and vanity and creating an "us against them" mentality. Once we go down that rabbit hole and find comfort in that kind of behavior, it becomes hard to see out, and the light grows dim. "By their fruit you will recognize them. Do people pick grapes from thornbushes, or figs from thistles? Likewise every good tree bears good fruit, but a bad tree bears bad fruit... Every tree that does not bear good fruit is cut down and thrown into the fire. Thus, by their fruit you will recognize them." (Matt 7:16-20) If you're not in the light or your eyes are closed you can't tell if the fruit is good, and you could find yourself biting into something that's really bad. The worst part is, if you swallow it and the seed grows, you will find *yourself* cut down and thrown into the fire! If you want to be in The Way, you have to check what they have boxed up and not buy the evil that is shined up to look good which is what these people are selling. As Adam and Eve found out, fruit on the outside can be tempting, look and sound good, but as you bite in and dig deeper, where does it take you? The fruit of the Spirit is distinctive and easy to discern. It's always good to the taste as well as good for you.

Why is it we believe what we do? Just because it was on the internet or TV, perhaps by someone with letters behind their name, or some powerful speaker pushing the right buttons? You know that it doesn't make it true. Saying it over and over again doesn't make it true either. TV "news" where they spend more time telling you what to think than the actual news, as well as social media platforms, have opened a Pandora's box of misinformation, divisiveness, lies, and hate. Have you ever seen a plant that has broken apart concrete? All it takes is a small seed in a tiny crack of a strong wall that takes root and starts to grow. Maybe some story or post about those "other" people that strikes a chord with us, proving they are wrong and we are right. Since we only see one side and we can act with anonymity, we think and say something we wouldn't say to someone's face, agreeing with the post. Because the computer sees it, now we are getting more of the same, more divisive ads, more poison. Or we spend more time watching that channel that tells us what we want to hear; it makes us feel good, so we exclude all of the others because of course, they are fake. The seed has now taken root, a crack in the wall develops, and before long it completely envelopes us. Before we know it, we are thinking, agreeing with, supporting, and even saying negative, hurtful things about others—but it's okay, because we're told, and we've convinced ourselves, that we're right and they need to know it. Over time, the small seed has forced its way in, grown, and broken down the once-strong wall. Satan and his army rush in, we miss the grace of GOD, and we completely lose sight of how we affect others. "See to it that no one falls short of the grace of God and that no bitter root grows up to cause trouble and defile many." (Heb 12:15) Something that starts so small, some hidden need or desire, can bring down and defile the strongest person. One small seed if allowed to grow will cause us to "fall short" and miss the grace of God entirely. "Each person is tempted when they are dragged away by their own evil desire and enticed. Then, after desire has conceived, it gives birth to sin; and sin, when it is full-grown, gives birth to death." (James 1:14-15) You're not alone; notice he includes "each one" that's all of us. There is no escaping temptation, not even for Jesus. "Because he himself suffered when he was tempted, he is able to help those who are being tempted." (Heb 2:18) Go to him for help.

The time to stop the temptation and kill the seed is when it is first planted, and before it takes root. The longer it grows the more it is at home and harder to even recognize as it spreads. After a while it takes over, and breaks down our wall. We take pride in it, eat its fruit, wallow in its foliage, and we don't even recognize it as a danger. We have an answer for everything. The problem is when it is the wrong answer from the wrong source.

What happens to our car or house if it's not maintained? Every so often every strong wall needs a good cleaning to remove those seeds and patch the cracks. There are a lot of weeds and seeds blowing around on the other side of our wall, and all it takes is the smallest of cracks for a seed to take hold. It shouldn't be surprising that what is evil can sound so good and so right. "Satan himself masquerades as an angel of light. It is not surprising, then, if his servants also masquerade as servants of righteousness. Their end will be what their actions deserve." (2 Cor 11:14-15) A root embedded in a strong wall can go deep and can become difficult to remove. If something, anything, no matter how good it feels or sounds, does not cause you to think and act out of love, agreeing with **both** the Spirit and the Word, it is not from God. Take the time and make the effort to remove it right away before it takes root. The better it makes you feel, the more important it is that you remove it quickly. Then fill the void in your wall with a higher love that comes from the Word, like mortar, before it does more damage.

If we want to avoid the end result with the kind of collapse that thinking this way is guaranteed to bring, we must test everything we take in and believe. "Dear friends, do not believe every spirit, but test the spirits to see whether they are from God" (1 John 4:1) Ask yourself, "Does it agree with God's Word? What influence does this have on me? How does it affect the heart?" Remove the seeds of discord and desire, or **anything** that is different from the Word of God, no matter what comfort it brings, or how good it sounds or makes us feel. Remove that which **we want**, clean out any damage it may have done so the repair will stick, and then smooth over the crack with a mixture of His truth, that which comes from His Word, and His love, the kind of love that Jesus wants of us. "Not everyone who says to me, 'Lord, Lord,' will enter the kingdom of heaven, but only the one who does the will of my Father who is in heaven." (Matt 7:21) The will of the Father should be obvious to us if we are truthful with ourselves. If you have a weed that has already taken hold, stop and pray now. Renounce it. Ask for the courage and the strength to cut it off at the source. A plant without water will die and its root comes out with ease. Remove all you can and then stop watering them. Only tend to plants that bring forth the kind of fruit worthy of a disciple of Jesus. Turn away from that which causes division and self-gratification, turn and face Jesus, and his love. "Now the works of the flesh are evident: sexual immorality, impurity, sensuality, idolatry, sorcery, [spiritism (that is, encouraging the activity of demons)] enmity, strife, jealousy, fits of anger, rivalries, dissensions, divisions, envy, drunkenness, orgies, and things like these. I warn you, as I warned you before, that those who do such things will not inherit the kingdom of God. But the fruit of the Spirit is love, joy, peace, patience, kindness, goodness, faithfulness, gentleness, self-control; against such things there is no law. And those who belong to Christ Jesus have crucified the flesh with its passions and desires. If we live by the Spirit, let us also walk by the Spirit." (Gal 5:19-25 ESV, [TLB]) How many people today seem to have forgotten this? If you have the Spirit of God in your heart then act like it, walk the walk. Avoid the trees and bushes that do not produce the fruit of the Spirit. If you want to get in shape change your diet. The trees you take shelter under and what you consume show in the way you live. How many are quick to anger, sow discord, quick to put others down, and are proud to be a part of this kind of group rather than show kindness, gentleness, and self-control? We have it backward—having self-control and showing kindness to everyone is not easy; it shows strength rather than weakness. Weakness is giving in to our base emotions. The challenge is to be truthful with ourselves and walk in the light even when the world is dark, and it's not easy.

"God is light; in him there is no darkness at all. If we claim to have fellowship with him and yet walk in the darkness, we lie and do not live by the truth. But if we walk in the light, as he is in the light, we have fellowship with one another, and the blood of Jesus, his Son, purifies us from all sin." (1 John 1:5-7) Trying to find happiness in this world through the things of this world will always disappoint. They often cause damage and death, and yet they are so attractive and powerful. Some of us are old enough to remember when everyone smoked cigarettes. We saw the death, the disease, and the pain it caused, and yet we also saw just how hard it was to quit. We thought the next generation would not have to go through this, and yet here we are with young people vaping. It seems as long as people are advertising, people are buying. "Light has come into the world, but people loved darkness instead of light" (John 3:19) And so it is with pride, division, anger, the "us against them" mentality, sensuality, and all the things listed, including spiritualism. When we try to find the creator, or power and happiness in this world through the spirit world, without submitting to, or going through Jesus, it will not end up well. There is power there for sure, but not all spirits are from above as the Scripture plainly states. "The Spirit clearly says that in later times some will abandon the faith and follow deceiving spirits and things taught by demons. Such teachings come through hypocritical liars, whose consciences have been seared as with a hot iron." (1 Tim 4:1-2) Many today take the name of Jesus while following those that are divisive and harsh without thought or realization of what they're doing. Any conscience they had is gone.

If you've ever seen a picture of the devil you know he has a tail, and it's in his tale that his power lies. Just because you haven't noticed a demon doesn't mean they aren't there, deceitful spirits and lies are everywhere around us. Demons don't need to force their way in with a lot of fanfare in order to possess you. They can spin your head around, change your voice, and control you without you even noticing. There is only one Spirit that is from GOD and sent from Jesus, all others need to be cut off and cast out. The easiest way for them to possess you is to get you to fall in love with the things of this world. "Do not love the world or the things in the world. If anyone loves the world, the love of the Father is not in him. For all that is in the world—the lust of the flesh, the lust of the eyes, and the pride of life—is not of the Father but is of the world. And the world is passing away, and the lust of it; but he who does the will of God abides forever." (1 John 2:15-17 NKJV)

Sometimes the "dark side," or what we know to be sin, seems like it would be a wonderful life. It can feel good to just put yourself first, just do whatever pleases you. Why care about anyone else, especially if they're not part of "your" group? Putting others down, excessive pride, doing drugs, getting drunk, partying, one night stands, talking smack, even just patting yourself on the back—they all feel wonderful at the time. If you're just doing what feels good today, right now, how will you feel tomorrow, when it's over? Want another fix? Then another? How far are you willing to go down that road, and where does it lead? Will it feel as good the tenth time, the hundredth time? Are you willing to pay the price? Once you fall into addictive behavior, whatever it is—not just alcohol and drugs, but relationships, anger toward others, narcissism, greed, pride, or being judgmental—whatever it may be, will that make you happy? And what kind of toll does that kind of life take? Are any addicts in general happy? Do you see a lot of joy in their life? Look around, find people who have been living that way for twenty, thirty years, or more—if you can. Then find someone who has quietly spent their life as a disciple of Jesus. Physically, emotionally, and energetically, how do they compare? Look at people who have been walking with the Almighty for a long time, following his Word, not just faking it, but living it day in and day out year after year. Which way looks like more fun now, and what does that tell you? "And we know that in all things God works for the good of those who love him, who have been called according to his purpose." (Rom 8:28) When his purpose is not our goal we are not whole, and as time goes by, it will take its toll.

There have been times when society listened to their natural moral compass that GOD instilled in us. There also have been times in history when people gradually moved away from morality and concluded that anything they desired was okay. We tell ourselves, "If it's in my heart it's natural and must be right; it's just who I am, the way I was born." Truth is that if there wasn't any pleasure in sin, it wouldn't be tempting, and the fact that we're all tempted by different things should not be surprising. I had a good friend and Gospel preacher named Dave that alcoholism ran in his family. It just seemed to be in their DNA. It was something he grew up with and saw in his family members. Not only in the older generations but also in his peers, both his own age and younger ones as well. There were far more members of his immediate family who were alcoholics than you would expect. Far more than other families around, and far more than the percentages found in the general public. Dave made the decision at a young age never to even taste anything alcoholic. He never preached that drinking alcohol in moderation was a sin, or stopped anyone else around him from having a drink. He was fine being with someone who had a beer with their pizza or a glass of wine with their pasta, but not him. He had made up his mind never to touch anything alcoholic, ever. Why take a chance? If he didn't like it, no loss. If he did, it could be devastating to everything he loved and stood for. His biggest fear was that he would like it, and we all know the problem is that when we like and want something, we can **always** find a way to justify it. He could say that if it's in his DNA he should go ahead and enjoy it. As long as it makes him happy and he doesn't hurt others, isn't it okay? After all, it's the way God made him. If it's the way you were born doesn't that make it okay? It's not a weakness, it's just who I am, my true self. After all, I've always had these desires; doesn't that make it right? Trying to change is hard, and why should I have to change? Who's to say the way God made me is wrong? People who don't accept me are the ones with a problem; they're just bigoted, self-righteous, and judgmental. While it doesn't justify anything, in some cases that maybe true. Everyone, all of us, have a battle to fight.

There was a time when being openly critical of others and agreeing with those who were, was seen as what it is; evil. People knew it was wrong and it was shared in hushed voices and only with someone close, or trustworthy, so no one else would know. To attempt to raise ourselves up by lowering others has nothing to do with love or respect and is not from above. Getting perverse pleasure from belittling others hurts the heart, destroys the conscience as much as any sin, and can cause actions that hurt the body as well as the soul. There are things in this life for which even the smallest bite of the apple will bring death. There are also many things that become a sin only with time and when they are taken in excess, when they are allowed to get between us and God. In many ways they bring the most danger. You can choose any path you want. If you choose to walk in The Way, you have to let GOD tell you what's right and what's wrong and not rationalize your desires and weaknesses. Love others, follow the Spirit, and live in its light, no matter what we feel or think or how hard it is to change. "In everything you do, stay away from complaining and arguing so that no one can speak a word of blame against you. You are to live clean, innocent lives as children of God in a dark world full of people who are crooked and stubborn. Shine out among them like beacon lights, holding out to them the Word of Life." (Phil 2:14-16 TLB) Complaining, name-calling, and arguing show depravity. I don't know about other generations, but this sure seems to fit today. Being a part of this kind of behavior just **can-not**, and does not, fit a child of GOD, under *any* condition. He calls on us to stand out as a beacon of light in the darkness, and show others the way.

"They perish because they refused to love the truth and so be saved. For this reason God sends them a powerful delusion so that they will believe the lie and so that all will be condemned

who have not believed the truth but have delighted in wickedness." (2 Thess 2:10-12) Do you know the powerful delusion
he is talking about? Have you seen it, and has it affected you?
They are called powerful not because the words contain power,
but because they are presented with power and draw people to
them, like a bug to a bug zapper. There are one or two powerful
delusions out there; avoid them at all costs! And don't avoid
one only to get caught up in another lie; you're better than that.

Chapter Ten
The Way to a Healthy Heart

"Create in me a pure heart, O God,
and renew a steadfast spirit within me.
Do not cast me from your presence or
take your Holy Spirit from me."
—Psalm. 51:10-11

We have a serious problem with heart disease, and it's not just in this country—it's everywhere. It is the leading cause of death worldwide, and again like two sides of a coin, it's both physical and spiritual. "Because of your stubbornness and your unrepentant heart, you are storing up wrath against yourself for the day of God's wrath, when his righteous judgment will be revealed." (Rom 2:5-6) Being stubborn, or determining in your heart not to change or repent is spiritual heart disease, and if left untreated, it will bring spiritual death. When we no longer listen to our heart we become cold and calloused. It becomes easy to hate, to see others as the enemy and the source of all our problems and to glory in putting people down. "Many false prophets will appear and deceive many people. Because of the increase of wickedness, the love of most will grow cold," (Matt 24:11-12) I have heard it said that when we are judged it won't be with a law book but a stethoscope. Doctors call it arrhythmia when the brain and the heart stop communicating as they should. It causes sudden cardiac arrest, and it causes over half of the deaths that come from heart disease.

The heart problem we are most familiar with is that of a heart attack or a stroke. The first heart attack is usually surviv-able and serves as a warning. It constantly causes pain and is caused by blocked arteries, the same as a stroke. Arteries do not become blocked overnight it happens slowly over time. Little by little, piece by piece until it hits us. The spiritual heart is no different. Over time we find reasons to become a little bit colder, a little more judgmental, calloused to sin and to others, and soon we block God out. "For this people's heart has become calloused; they hardly hear with their ears, and they have closed their eyes." (Matt 13:15) We all know that to have a healthy heart, diet and exercise are two things we can do to improve our heart health. I had an uncle who on his wife's side of the family had a history of small arteries and heart problems. All of his wife's brothers and sisters were careful with their diet. He was a successful and hard-working farmer with a larger-than-life personality who was also stubborn. Even though his wife warned him, he would still make fun of her and her family while drinking whole milk and eating the fattest cuts of meat almost every meal, because that's where the flavor was. He finally had a massive stroke that left him angry, suffering, and bedridden until he died.

Our spiritual diet can do the same to us. Are we just consuming what has the most flavor, that which we enjoy the most? Some video games, porn, TV, radio, and media stations that spew hate, negativity, pride, and lies masquerading as truth? That's exactly what a lot of people are consuming today, and it is restricting the life-giving love of God to both the heart and the mind. It's also easy to become a spiritual couch potato. It's easier to just keep your mouth shut and not say anything. They say not to talk about religion or politics. Maybe it's time to stop talking about religion and start talking about what GOD and Jesus have done and can do in our life. "His word is in my heart like a fire, a fire shut up in my bones. I am weary of holding it in; indeed, I cannot." (Jer. 20:9) If we are "holding it in," is it even there? In either case, it is a warning and a sure sign of heart trouble.

The best way to light the fire is to be around others who have the same fire. If we are to keep the fire stoked it needs fuel and oxygen. The fuel comes from his Word and the oxygen comes from getting up and moving. Everywhere we turn there are talking heads blowing smoke and we all should know the kind of damage to our heart caused by sitting around and sucking in that kind of smoke. Studies have been done, and it seems to be true, that 80 to 90 percent of church work is done by 10 to 20 percent of the people. Imagine what could happen if that percentage was higher and more of us got off the couch, stood up, and spoke up for our faith.

Sometimes our heart breaks. Things don't go the way we wish they would, and words can-not describe the pain we feel. It's then that we need GOD the most. "He will be gracious if you ask for help. He will surely respond to the sound of your cries. Though the Lord gave you adversity for food and suffering for drink, he will still be with you to teach you… Right behind you a voice will say, "This is the way you should go," (Isa 30:19-21 NLT) We have to learn; learn to listen, and learn to walk in The Way.

When I was learning to water-ski over a jump ramp I was told not to look down because you will go where you look. Sure enough, as soon as I cleared the ramp the natural reaction took over. I looked down and wound up doing a belly flop. Some lessons it seems you just have to learn the hard way. It only took once for me to learn my lesson. After that, I kept my head up, looked ahead, and began to soar higher as well as longer and longer distances. The same thing is true in our spiritual life. "So we fix our eyes not on what is seen, but on what is unseen, since what is seen is temporary, but what is unseen is eternal." (2 Cor 4:18) There are going to be storms in life for all of us;

it's just a fact of life. There is only one place we need to fix our eyes on and one way to stay strong. "Therefore everyone who hears these words of mine and puts them into practice is like a wise man who built his house on the rock. The rain came down, the streams rose, and the winds blew and beat against that house; yet it did not fall, because it had its foundation on the rock." (Matt 7:24-25) Letting go of "our way," listening to Jesus, having his Spirit, and putting His words into practice will give us the foundation we need to withstand the storms that we face and be the best pain killer you can get. Although it's true; this pain killer is habit-forming, and can even be even addictive.

The effect that stress has on our heart is well-known and well-documented. Stress affects not only our heart but also every aspect of our lives. Stress affects our immune systems making us more susceptible to disease and even colds. Stress also affects our thinking, making us more likely to be depressed and therefore it affects our spiritual lives and our relationship with God as well. It doesn't matter what race you are or skin tone you have, if you're super rich or dirt poor, insightful or oblivious, it's just part of how we're made. Worry and stress are there for a reason. It kept our ancestors from choosing a cave too close to a lion's den and can give us that extra push to be successful when we need it. It raises the blood pressure and adrenaline which is exactly why we can't live in that state except for short periods of time. If not managed stress becomes a killer of both body and soul. God does not want you to live in a state of anxiety and stress but rather to learn to trust Him.

Learning to deal with stress is one of the most important things you will ever do, and that's true for every one of us. Studies show the relationship between stress and disease is affected by the nature, number, and persistence of the stress as well as by the individual's biological vulnerability and learned patterns of coping.[1] The first thing I get from this is that coping with stress is harder for some than others but necessary for all of us. The second thing is that sometimes we have to remove ourselves from a stressful situation. There was a person who was close to me when I was young who became very successful in business and also a strong Christian. He was running two departments of a large and successful computer company; he flew all around the country, and even to other countries—until he had a heart attack. Fortunately, it was a warning. His cardiologist told him he was going to retire, either to a place of his choosing or at the cemetery. As it turned out he discovered that he already had enough money to walk away from his job, and that God had other plans for him. Sometimes in life, we get a notice that a change and a new direction is required.

The third, and perhaps the most important, is that we need to have a learned pattern of coping with stress. As luck would have it Jesus gave us the pattern, and it's up to us to learn it.

"I tell you not to worry about everyday life—whether you have enough food and drink, or enough clothes to wear.

---

[1] NIH National Library of Medicine; STRESS AND HEALTH: Psychological, Behavioral, and Biological Determinants

Isn't life more than food, and your body more than clothing? Look at the birds. They don't plant or harvest or store food in barns, for your heavenly Father feeds them. And aren't you far more valuable to him than they are? Can all your worries add a single moment to your life? And why worry about your clothing? Look at the lilies of the field and how they grow. They don't work or make their clothing, yet Solomon in all his glory was not dressed as beautifully as they are. And if God cares so wonderfully for wildflowers that are here today and thrown into the fire tomorrow, he will certainly care for you. Why do you have so little faith? "So don't worry about these things, saying, 'What will we eat? What will we drink? What will we wear?' These things dominate the thoughts of unbelievers, but your heavenly Father already knows all your needs. Seek the Kingdom of God above all else, and live righteously, and he will give you everything you need. So don't worry about tomorrow, for tomorrow will bring its own worries. Today's trouble is enough for today." (Matt 6:25-34 NLT)

When stress and worry are a part of our everyday life we are not trusting in GOD. We are in the same boat as those who are negative and not acting out of love. GOD requires of us to let go of the physical, walk in faith, and trust him. "We live by faith, not by sight." (2 Cor 5:7-8) Whenever you put pressure on something, whether it's an apple or an orange whatever comes out is always the same—whatever is on the inside. When pressure and stress come along, having love on the inside will turn a bad situation into a positive one. Relationships change, and everything in this world wears out or breaks at some point. Instead of worrying about it remember that with God's help there is always a way forward. Things can always be repaired, fixed, or replaced, and even death was overcome by Christ.

After my dad passed away, my mother remarried a wonderful, warm, and loving man who had just lost his wife. Although it was put to the test when my dad died, my mother always believed that a strong faith would carry you through anything in life. Then her second husband developed Alzheimer's. As the disease progressed, it didn't take long before she realized she couldn't make it on her own. Love and faith in God, no matter how strong, wasn't enough without help. "Carry each other's burdens, and in this way you will fulfill the law of Christ." (Gal:6 2)

We can rely on God and still need to make changes in our life as well as depend upon others. It is the way God made us, and there is no shame or lack of faith to admit it. When things fall apart, be at peace. Take some time to worship the Father and feel the presence of the Spirit within you. Learn to let go of all the little stuff in life, one at a time. Worry just a little less every day and remember, to your God—it's all little stuff. "Peace I leave with you; my peace I give you. I do not give to you as the world gives. Do not let your hearts be troubled and do not be afraid." (Jn 14:27)

What is it that troubles your heart? How many things do you have that make you anxious? What causes you worry? I'm not talking about the silly little things that will never happen, but rather real concerns, things you need to be on top of. If they are important enough to watch out for then they are important enough to be listed. Take a minute to write them down; let's get them out in the open where we can deal with them, name them, and face them. Don't leave them floating around in your subconscious where they can pop up and attack without warning causing stress and worry. Instead, let's make sure they get the attention they deserve and are dealt with properly. Get a pad of paper, then get them out of the recesses of your conscience where they like to hang out, and place them front and center. Take a minute to think about it. Include everything and don't leave anything out. You can even include some of the silly little things just for fun if you want. Better to be safe than sorry; who knows? They could happen if the conditions were just right. It should only take a little while. Go ahead; I'll wait.

Okay, now that you have your list, it's time to turn them over to someone who has the power to actually take care of them. You know you don't; after all, you have already tried. Others can sometimes give some comfort but they don't have the power needed to make them go away. There is someone who looks at the things on your list as if they are as easy as child's play, and the good news is that he's excited to help you. All you have to do is hand them over! "Give all your worries and cares to God, for he cares about you." (1 Pet. 5:7 NLT) When he says to "give" them to God, that's exactly what he means. If you give something away, that means you no longer have it. Once handed over, they are his and no longer yours to worry about or fret over. If you still have them, that means God doesn't, so it's time to send them off. You don't need an envelope, proper postage, an address, (hint—it's not at the North Pole), or even an email address. He has a secure private server with a GPS up-link. Remember that when your spirit was placed in you it included an app with a direct link hardwired in. Close down all the distractions, find a quiet place, and follow the directions. "But you, when you pray, go into your room, and when you have shut your door, pray to your Father who is in the secret place; and your Father who sees in secret will reward you openly." (Matt. 6:6 NKJV) We all have a secret place, a communication room; it is a very comfortable place built for two. Once you have found it, you can relax and surround yourself with the glory of a masterful and loving Father who has the power to easily take care of all your issues. Everything from the most pressing worries to the silly little things. Once something makes the list it can be sent directly from your heart to His. Remember that your exact words don't matter because Jesus sent a Translator[2] and a Comforter to take care of that.

Once you are finished your list carries no importance anymore. It's like the first draft of a presentation. Once given, it can be tossed or placed in a file that you can look back on like a history book. GOD is smarter than you; he knows more,

---

[2] "We do not know what we ought to pray for, but the Spirit himself intercedes for us with groans that words cannot express. And he who searches our hearts knows the mind of the Spirit, because the Spirit intercedes for the saints in accordance with God's will." Rom 8:26-27

including the hearts of everyone around you, as well as what their needs are, and he will make it work out for the best.[3] You don't have to understand everything, that's His job, and he's good at it. You can let it go and be at peace, because it's over and done with. "Do not be anxious about anything, but in every situation, by prayer and petition, with thanksgiving, present your requests to God. And the peace of God, which transcends all understanding, will guard your hearts and your minds in Christ Jesus."(Phil 4:6-7) You can be brave and even bold in every situation because, through Jesus, GOD is guarding your heart and mind.

Once you've found your secret place you can visit as often as you would like. Future requests, guidance, wisdom, forgiveness, direction, what you should do, where you should go, you can even ask how things are going with that problem you gave him—anything that is on your mind and makes the list. Cool thing is that you can take as long as you want. He created time and he can always make more for you.

The last heart issue I want to talk about are the valves. When they don't function and seal tight, we lose energy and are unable to function as we should. Both what goes into our heart and what comes out is important. "A good man produces good deeds from a good heart. And an evil man produces evil deeds from his hidden wickedness. Whatever is in the heart

---

[3] "And we know that in all things God works for the good of those who love him, who have been called according to his purpose." Rom. 8:28

overflows into speech." (Luke 6:45 TLB) Many people think it's admirable to "say it like it is" and just let anything out they may be thinking without regard, like a leaky valve. It's not. "Be wise in the way you act toward outsiders; make the most of every opportunity. Let your conversation be always full of grace, seasoned with salt, so that you may know how to answer everyone." (Col 4:5-6) Being offensive, putting others down, exalting your opinions, not listening, and always talking about yourself—these are signs of a narcissist and someone foolish, not a disciple of Jesus or someone who has God in their life. We're lucky, the only way to repair a physical heart valve is with surgery; however, a spiritual heart valve can be repaired by just stopping and listening to yourself, to the words coming out of your mouth, and by watching the actions you take. It can feel good to tell someone off who deserves it, but is it wise? What is the end result you are looking for—just to feel good at the moment or to feel good in the long term and walk in The Way?

Chapter Eleven

The Way to Die

The last coin and its two sides are the biggest, most important, most valuable, and most powerful of any and all. Yet few, if any, of the popular churches that are of any size, the best-selling authors, or those on TV ever speak of it anymore. Or if they do it's only one side of the coin, so it doesn't offend anyone. Whether you want to acknowledge it or not doesn't matter; it will happen just the way it's written, and *you* will be there!

"Then I saw a great white throne and him who was seated on it. The earth and the sky fled from his presence, and there was no place for them. And I saw the dead, great and small, standing before the throne, and books were opened. Another book was opened, which is the book of life. The dead were judged according to what they had done as recorded in the books. The sea gave up the dead that were in it, and death and Hades gave up the dead that were in them, and each person was judged according to what they had done. Then death and Hades were thrown into the lake of fire. The lake of fire is the second death. Anyone whose name was not found written in the book of life was thrown into the lake of fire." (Rev 20:11-15)

I'm sorry if any of this makes you uncomfortable, it should, either for yourself or for someone you know, but that doesn't make it any less true. We will all see exactly what is described here, both you and me, our friends, our family, everybody who has ever lived or is yet to be born. It doesn't matter how great you are, or think you are, or how small and insignificant you see yourself; whether you choose to believe it or not, you will be there. "For we must all appear before the judgment seat of Christ, so that each of us may receive what is due us for the things done while in the body, whether good or bad." (2 Cor 5:10) What you do matters. What is in your heart matters. What you think on matters, and being prepared for death, it matters—a lot.

There are those who take death lightheartedly. Some talk about past lives, the way other religions teach. However, the Bible does not. "Just as people are destined to die once, and after that to face judgment, so Christ was sacrificed once to take away the sins of many people; and he will appear a second time, not to bear sin, but to bring salvation to those who are waiting for him." (Heb 9:27-28) But even if it were somehow true that we have lived past lives, what makes you think that you, or anyone else, will have another? Why would anyone even want another life? The only reason anyone would want to live on this earth again is because they know they are not ready for judgment. If you were ready, you would be "waiting for him" and looking forward to seeing Jesus and being with the Father. "For to me, to live is Christ and to die is gain." (Phil 1:21-22) Near-death experiences do not negate judgment. What happens in the first few minutes after a body shuts down does not tell the whole story any more than the first few minutes of a long trip tell about the journey or the destination. If anything, all those experiences show is that consciousness continues after life ends. I think we all know there has been only one who died, was buried in a tomb over the course of three days without any medical treatment, and then returned. Ironically he is the only one who knew where he was going and what was going to happen. I'm thinking we should probably take the time to listen to him.

Just a few days before Jesus was crucified he said; "When the Son of Man comes in his glory, and all the angels with him, he will sit on his glorious throne. All the nations will be gathered before him, and he will separate the people one from another as a shepherd separates the sheep from the goats. He will put the sheep on his right and the goats on his left. "Then the King will say to those on his right, 'Come, you who are blessed by my Father; take your inheritance, the kingdom prepared for you since the creation of the world. For I was hungry and you gave me something to eat, I was thirsty and you gave me something to drink, I was a stranger and you invited me in, I needed clothes and you clothed me, I was sick and you looked after me, I was in prison and you came to visit me.'

"Then the righteous will answer him, 'Lord, when did we see you hungry and feed you, or thirsty and give you something to drink? When did we see you a stranger and invite you in, or needing clothes and clothe you? When did we see you sick or in prison and go to visit you?' "The King will reply, 'Truly I tell you, whatever you did for one of the least of these brothers and sisters of mine, you did for me.' "Then he will say to those on his left, 'Depart from me, you who are cursed, into the eternal fire prepared for the devil and his angels. For I was hungry and you gave me nothing to eat, I was thirsty and you gave me nothing to drink, I was a stranger and you did not invite me in, I needed clothes and you did not clothe me, I was sick and in prison and you did not look after me.' "They also will answer, 'Lord, when did we see you hungry or thirsty or a stranger or needing clothes or sick or in prison, and did not help you?' "He will reply, 'Truly I tell you, whatever you did not do for one of the least of these, you did not do for me.' "Then they will go away to eternal punishment, but the righteous to eternal life." (Matt 25:31-46)

Those in this Scripture who he sent away to eternal punishment are not people who did not know Jesus, or didn't believe in him. These were people that called themselves Christians, fully believing they were under God's grace and following Jesus. "For the time is come that judgment must begin at the house of God: and if it first begin at us, what shall the end be of them that obey not the gospel of God? And if the righteous scarcely be saved, where shall the ungodly and the sinner appear?" (1 Peter 4:17-18 KJV) Did you notice that the bar is not set at being a good person or even believing in Jesus? It is quite clear: "them that obey not the gospel of God." These are those of us who know, or should know the Gospel, but for one reason or another, they just can't find it within themselves to give God complete control and obey it. Do you believe? Great! For heaven's sake don't stop there; keep going, and put your faith into action.

A while back I saw where three people went off into the Colorado wilderness to live "off-grid" in a tent with very little in the way of provisions or preparation, despite their family and friends trying to talk them out of it.[1] As you probably guessed, their "mummified" bodies were discovered by hikers in the spring. The natural reaction is to think that was pretty dumb, and gee, who couldn't see that coming? We all know that when we move or even take a trip, we have to plan for it. It kind of goes without saying that if you don't, you're asking for trouble, or in this case much worse. If we know we need to plan even for a weekend trip, how much more for a long one, the trip of a lifetime, one that will last an eternity, a permanent move?

[1] LA times 8/2023

It has been said that heaven is a prepared place for a prepared people. Just before Jesus was arrested and taken away to be crucified he said, "Do not let your hearts be troubled. You believe in God; believe also in me. My Father's house has many rooms; if that were not so, would have told you I am going there to prepare a place for you? And if I go and prepare a place for you, I will come back and take you to be with me that you also may be where I am. You know the way to the place where I am going." Thomas said to him, "Lord, we don't know where you are going, so how can we know the way?" Jesus answered, "I am the way and the truth and the life." (John 14:1-6) Jesus is prepared for those who follow him. The better you know Jesus the better you know The Way, and the better prepared you are for Jesus. Don't you just love the way your GPS tells you to turn just as you pass the intersection? By listening to, and following Jesus, you can avoid wrong turns and false teachers on the way to an easy move: an eternal life that's better than anything you can imagine.

"Then I saw a new heaven and a new earth, for the first heaven and the first earth had passed away, and there was no longer any sea. I saw the Holy City, the new Jerusalem, coming down out of heaven from God, prepared as a bride beautifully dressed for her husband. And I heard a loud voice from the throne saying, "Look the dwelling of God is among the people, and he will dwell with them. They will be his people, and God himself will be with them and be their God. He will wipe every tear from their eyes. There will be no more death or mourning

or crying or pain, for the old order of things has passed away."
(Rev 21:1-4) You and I have an opportunity to live in a second
Garden of Eden if you will, one new and improved, *far* better
than the original.

The apostle John continues on: "And he carried me away
in the Spirit to a mountain great and high, and showed me the
Holy City, Jerusalem, coming down out of heaven from God.
It shone with the glory of God, and its brilliance was like that
of a very precious jewel, like a jasper, clear as crystal... And the
city [was made] of pure gold, as pure as glass. The foundations
of the city walls were decorated with every kind of precious
stone...The twelve gates were twelve pearls, each gate made of
a single pearl. The great street of the city was of gold, as pure
as transparent glass. I did not see a temple in the city, because
the Lord God Almighty and the Lamb are its temple. The city
does not need the sun or the moon to shine on it, for the glory
of God gives it light, and the Lamb is its lamp. The nations
will walk by its light, and the kings of the earth will bring their
splendor into it. On no day will its gates ever be shut, for there
will be no night there. The glory and honor of the nations
will be brought into it. Nothing impure will ever enter it, nor
will anyone who does what is shameful or deceitful, but only
those whose names are written in the Lamb's book of life." (Rev
21:10-27) For those who have their name in the "Lamb's book
of life" heaven is beyond anything you could possibly imagine.

Years ago when I was preaching at a small congregation, a
quite literal "little old lady" who had spent her life as a devout

disciple of the LORD was told she didn't have long to live. She came up to me and asked, "What happens when you die?" I began to talk about some of the Scriptures I've used here when she stopped me and said, "Yeah, yeah, yeah, I know all of that, but what *really* happens?" There was no use to insult her and avoid the question; I knew exactly what she meant. So I told her I would look into it and pray about it and get back to her next Sunday. That week I prayed and reread all the Scriptures on the subject again, looking for anything I might have missed, but there was nothing there. It was only after I had finished and still had nothing, that my daughter came running up to my chair, calling out to me in that happy child's voice that the light came on. It was clear; it's the same way you answer nearly all difficult questions. Think of the Majestic Almighty LORD GOD, Ruler of Heaven and Earth, the Alpha and the Omega, Creator, and Master of the Universe—simply as our Father.

The next Sunday as soon as service was over, I had just barely stepped down from the podium when she came running up with only one word: "Well?" "Think back and remember when you were a little girl and Christmas was coming," I said. "One day, a large and very special package appears under the tree. You look and sure enough it has your name on it! You run to your father and ask repeatedly pulling on his shirt "What is it?!" But he just smiles and says "It's something very special from me to you. I know you very well, and I made it just for you. I know you will really like it," he says with a smile. So you ask again "But what is it?" He kneels down, looks at you with love, smiles and laughs a little, and then gives you some hints and clues of what it's like so you can think about it and guess. But no matter how many times you ask, he just tells you that you will just have to wait until the day comes that you can open it. "That's what it's like," I said. A big smile had already come across her face, and I could feel the weight lift and joy settle in on her as she looked up at me, and simply said, "Thank you." Then still smiling she turned and walked away. A little over a month later I performed a graveside service for her family. "No eye has seen, no ear has heard, no mind has imagined what God has prepared for those who love him." (1 Cor 2:9)

"And He who sits on the throne said, "Behold, I am making all things new." And He said, "Write, for these words are faithful and true." Then He said to me, "It is done. I am the Alpha and the Omega, the beginning and the end. I will give to the one who thirsts from the spring of the water of life without cost. "He who overcomes will inherit these things, and I will be his God and he will be My son. "But for the cowardly and unbelieving and abominable and murderers and immoral persons and sorcerers and idolaters and all liars, their part will be in the lake that burns with fire and brimstone, which is the second death." (Rev 21:5-8 NASU) GOD was *very* clear. Where you will spend eternity comes down to something as simple as whether you are able to "overcome," or whether you are "cowardly." But what does it mean to overcome? Overcome what? Only you know the answer to the question. If you are honest with yourself, you know exactly what GOD himself, seated on the throne, is talking about. I can't tell you what it is, or what steps to take, because it's different for you than it is for me. What you find easy can be a struggle for me, and the other way around as well, but we both know that GOD knows and understands.

If you're ready, I'm guessing you already have a pretty good idea of exactly what needs to be done; you just need the courage to follow through and the strength to continue. We also know that this is not a one-time battle but a war that is fought on multiple fronts. I do know that the more battles won the stronger we become. However, Satan is well-known for falling back, regrouping, and attacking again. Usually attacking stronger than before and when we least expect it. We can never back down, because that's the way the war is won—one battle at a time. One thing is the same for all of us: overcoming requires change. Change in commitment, in the way we think, and in the way we act. Often times something as simple as making even a small change is often the hardest part of the battle. At the same time even a small change, or a simple course correction early on, can prevent battles and make our life a whole lot easier later. If we are walking in The Way that means we're moving. Going forward requires first learning from the Spirit, and the Word he gave us, and then applying it to our lives. The devil loves it when we become spiritual couch potatoes, comfortable with the way we are, resisting change, taking the coward's way out. Oh sure, it's easy now, but the consequences can be devastating. Just as words can not describe how amazing heaven is, words can not describe just how horrible hell is.

There are two words in the Scriptures that are often translated as "hell." The first is *Hades*[2] in Greek, which comes from *Sheol* in Hebrew. While we often use it in a negative way it simply means "the unseen" or "the grave." It is the waiting place of the dead, the place we all go, the place Jesus went when he was crucified and died. "Concerning the resurrection of the Christ, that His soul was not left in Hades" (Acts 2:31 NKJV") The other word is *Gehenna*[3] which comes from the Valley of Gehenna or Hinnom which was a rocky and steep ravine southwest of Jerusalem. It was a place that in the past saw children sacrificed to idols, and it now served as a dump and sewer. Both filth and dead animals, (remember, they practiced animal sacrifice) were cast in and burned in the ever-present smoldering fire. This was not someplace anyone would go to for a picnic. This was the place Jesus used to depict where the devil and his angels, as well as the ungodly, the unbeliever, and those who simply do not obey him, will spend eternity. It's often referred to as the "lake of fire" for good reason.

Did you notice in Revelation chapter 21 when he was talking about those headed to the "fiery lake," that he started with the cowardly and ended with all liars? If you think that

---

[2] Hell: #86 haides (hah'-dace); from NT:1 (as negative particle) and NT:1492; properly, unseen, i.e. "Hades" or the place (state) of departed souls:
[3] Hell #1067 geena (gheh'-en-nah); of Hebrew origin [OT:1516 and OT:2011]; valley of (the son of) Hinnom; ge-henna (or Ge-Hinnom), a valley of Jerusalem, used (figuratively) as a name for the place (or state) of everlasting punishment:

it's okay to deliberately sin, just a little, because of his grace and the fact that GOD has forgiven us, you need to think again. "If we deliberately keep on sinning after we have received the knowledge of the truth, no sacrifice for sins is left, but only a fearful expectation of judgment and of raging fire that will consume the enemies of God. Anyone who rejected the law of Moses died without mercy on the testimony of two or three witnesses. How much more severely do you think someone deserves to be punished who has trampled the Son of God under foot, who has treated as an unholy thing the blood of the covenant that sanctified them, and who has insulted the Spirit of grace? For we know him who said, "It is mine to avenge; I will repay," and again, "The Lord will judge his people." It is a dreadful thing to fall into the hands of the living God." (Heb 10:26-31) We only want to think of the Almighty as a God of love, and he definitely is that, and his grace is very real, but don't mistake love for stupidity. "Do not be deceived, God is not mocked; for whatever a man sows, that he will also reap." (Gal. 6:7 NKJV) Love rejected is love denied. How would you feel if you gave someone you cared for a very special and expensive gift only to go by later and see it thrown out in the garbage? How do you think Jesus feels when his gift of love that he paid dearly for is tossed aside and rejected? Have you ever had your heart really broken? That's just a glimpse of how Jesus feels when we reject him.

We too often forget just the way GOD sees sin. "The wrath of God is being revealed from heaven against all the godlessness and wickedness of men who suppress the truth by their wickedness," (Rom 1:18-19) What do you suppose the wrath of someone so powerful would look like? Did you catch that phrase "suppress the truth"? Let it sink in a little bit. What does it mean to suppress the truth? Does it include not being the example we should be, or not speaking up when we should? What about holding back, keeping it inside, when someone is being divisive or spreading lies, twisting the truth, and misrepresenting the words of truth? When we are silent, are we suppressing the truth? What are we afraid of? Their anger? Being branded as one who dares to speak up for the way Jesus taught? Could that be enough to put us in this group? Personally, I don't know, and I don't want to find out the hard way. "Whoever acknowledges me before others, I will also acknowledge before my Father in heaven. But whoever disowns me before others, I will disown before my Father in heaven." (Matt 10:32-33) If we are silent and can't even acknowledge Jesus now, will he be silent and not even acknowledge us before the Father? Imagine you're standing before the throne of GOD in judgment this very moment, right now. Your whole life, your actions, words, and even your thoughts, both good and bad, are laid out for all to see before the Almighty God of Heaven and Earth—and Jesus remains silent. I don't know about you, but I have been guilty of being silent when I should have spoken up, and the thought, or even just the possibility, is enough to send shivers down my spine, and it helps to give me the strength to speak up next time! Even if the words come out all wrong or different than I want them to (as they almost always do) at least this time they will come out; and with practice I've got a good chance of doing better the next time, and maybe even helping someone. Who knows—it could happen. However, the one thing we can be sure of, is that it means more than just holding the Gospel in. There is no doubt he is talking about being the one who spreads a lie or turns away from the truth for whatever reason. Especially anyone who persuades others to follow a path that is different from the way that Christ taught by distorting or twisting the truth and not acting out of love, compassion, and humility. "Ignorant and unstable people distort, as they do the other Scriptures, to their own destruction. Therefore, dear friends, since you have been forewarned, be on your guard so that you may not be carried away by the error of the lawless and fall from your secure position." (2 Peter 3:16-17) Yes, we can have a secure position, and yes, we can still fall from it. Know that when we stop putting Jesus first, and start listening to other people, getting caught up and carried away by those who are distorting the truth, we fall. Know that we are taking GOD's place when we judge others, stopping and suppressing the Gospel by hardening others' hearts as well as our own. Do you remember the Scripture "You reap what you sow"? [4] "For the wages of sin is death, but the gift of God is eternal life in Christ Jesus our Lord." (Rom 6:23) More often than not twisting

---

[4] Gal 6:7 Do not be deceived: God cannot be mocked. A man reaps what he sows.

and distorting the truth, involves just focusing on one side of the coin rather than being open and wise, looking at all sides. A half-truth is still a lie.

"But about that day no one knows, not even the angels in heaven, nor the Son, but only the Father...Therefore keep watch, because you do not know on what day your Lord will come. But understand this: If the owner of the house had known at what time of night the thief was coming, he would have kept watch and would not have let his house be broken into. So you also must be ready, because the Son of Man will come at an hour when you do not expect him." (Matt 24:36 & 42-44) It's truly amazing to me that people spend their time trying to find out when the world will end, like there's some secret code hidden somewhere, instead of spending their time making sure they are ready for it. Pretending that "all dogs go to heaven," meaning that everybody, regardless of what they've believed or done, will enter heaven, is just foolish. You simply **can-not** believe in Jesus and think this way. Sorry, but you're only hurting yourself and those around you that you are not sharing the Gospel with—*urgently.*

Jesus was very clear: "Enter through the narrow gate. For wide is the gate and broad is the road that leads to destruction, and many enter through it. But small is the gate and narrow the road that leads to life, and only a few find it." (Matt 7:13-14) The cruelest thing you can do to someone is give false hope about something so important as an afterlife that lasts for eternity. If you love or care at all for someone, you need to share the Gospel with them right away, *now!* But do it with love, gentleness, and respect, no matter how hard it is, or what the consequences may be. Tell them your story, what God has done for you, or give them a copy of this book—whatever you need to do, do it right away, because the future is coming faster than ever.

"But the day of the Lord will come like a thief. The heavens will disappear with a roar;[5] the elements[6] will be destroyed[7] by fire, and the earth and everything in it will be laid bare. Since everything will be destroyed in this way, what kind of people ought you to be? You ought to live holy and godly lives as you look forward to the day of God and speed its coming. That day will bring about the destruction of the heavens by fire, and the elements will melt in the heat." (2 Peter 3:10-12) The planets, stars, and galaxies, all gone in an instant. And don't even try to change the meaning by changing the definitions. This word translated as roar means a whizzing sound, or with a crash, and when he says the elements, he is not referring to the periodic table. This word means things that were put in order. That's not just buildings and bridges, but rather your

---

[5] Roar. #4500; rhoizedon (hroyd-zay-don'); adverb from a derivative of rhoizos (a whir); whizzingly, i.e. with a crash:

[6] Elements. While it applies, this is referring to more than the periodic table. #4747 stoicheion (stoy-khi'-on); something orderly in arrangement, i.e. (by implication) a serial (basal, fundamental, initial) constituent (literally), proposition (figuratively):

[7] destroyed #3089; luo (loo'-o); a primary verb; to "loosen" (literally or figuratively);

DNA, molecules, and even the very atoms by which this world is made, **everything** that GOD put into order at creation. When he says destroyed, it means loosened or dissembled, that's the heavens, the earth, all of it. Everything that was put in order, all of it will be dissembled with a crash, making a literal earth-shattering whizzing sound. As sure as we live and breathe, that day is coming. "For we will all stand before God's judgment seat. It is written: 'As surely as I live,' says the Lord, every knee will bow before me; every tongue will acknowledge God.' So then, each of us will give an account of ourselves to God." (Rom 14:12 also see Isa. 45:23) There are no exceptions, no delays, and no appeals.

There is only one way to have your sins forgiven, and there is only one way to save yourself from Gehenna, the lake of fire. "If we say we have fellowship with him while we walk in darkness, we lie and do not practice the truth. But if we walk in the light, as he is in the light, we have fellowship with one another, and the blood of Jesus his Son cleanses us from all sin. If we say we have no sin, we deceive ourselves." (1 John 1:6-8 ESV) There is absolutely nothing more important than putting on Jesus and being "clothed"(Gal 3:27) in Him."(Rom 8:1) Have the faith (Heb 11:6) in Jesus to humble yourself and bury the old life in baptism, then rise to a new life, (Rom 6:4-5) and remain in him. Then walk every day in the light (Jn 8:12) as he is in the light, purified from all mistakes and sins (Jn 1:7) so that we remain in that "secure position."(2 Pet 3:17) I know that change can be a really, really, hard thing and that many may be telling you that you don't need it. I pray with all I have that you have the courage to "overcome," not being influenced in any way by anyone, especially by those who are divisive or suppress the truth. Set aside false concepts and listen to GOD alone. Put His Word first so that you are able to make whatever changes are necessary. "The Lord is not slow in keeping his promise, as some understand slowness. Instead he is patient with you, not wanting anyone to perish, but everyone to come to repentance." (2 Peter 3:9) You know The Way. There really is no reason to take any chances, make up your mind to experience the joy of living life His way.

"Therefore encourage one another and build up one another...Live in peace with one another. We urge you, brethren, admonish the unruly, encourage the fainthearted, help the weak, be patient with everyone. See that no one repays another with evil for evil, but always seek after that which is good for one another and for all people. Rejoice always; pray without ceasing; in everything give thanks; for this is God's will for you in Christ Jesus. Do not quench the Spirit...examine everything carefully; hold fast to that which is good; abstain from every form of evil. Now may the God of peace Himself sanctify you entirely; and may your spirit and soul and body be preserved complete, without blame at the coming of our Lord Jesus Christ." (1Thes 5:11-23 NASU)

Chapter Twelve

The Way to Knowledge

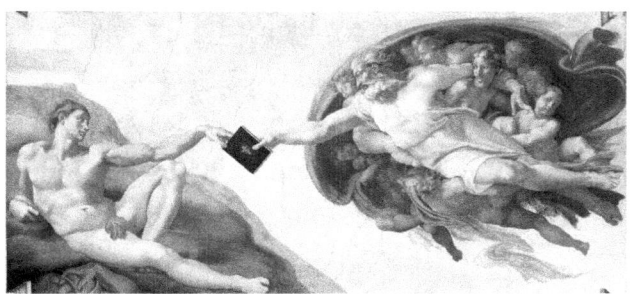

If an angel or messenger from God appeared to you, called you by name, and proclaimed, "You are special and chosen. GOD, the timeless all powerful creator of all that was, is, and is to come, loves *you*! I bring a special message from him because he wants you to be close to him. It will show you The Way so that you can live in happiness and peace. It will also guide you so you can avoid hell and spend an eternity in heaven with him when your life is over." Would you say "Okay thanks, when I get some time I'll check it out" and then set it down or put it on the shelf and go about what you were doing? Maybe just decide to let someone else read it and then tell you about it, since they probably know more and whatever they say is good? Would you just read a few sentences and say, "That's nice, but that's enough"? Would you skip over some parts because you don't believe that!? "I'll just read and focus on the parts that I like." Sound crazy? After all, who would do that knowing who it was from and what was at stake?? Reading the Bible with an open mind is pretty much the most important thing you will do in your life. But where do you start? I know that with all the different parts, or books, it can look daunting and seem complicated. Even if you've attended church for years knowing where to go or what to read can be hard. So, whether you're a long-time Bible student or it's your first time, I hope this outline of the New Testament is a useful resource and will be of some help.

The Story of Jesus

The first four books of the New Testament are called the Gospel, or Good News. From birth to death, they tell the story of Jesus, what he did, and what he taught. No doubt, much was written; however, these remain and were chosen to survive and then placed here for a reason. It should also be noted that the writers deemed it more important to put the teachings and works of Jesus together rather than in strict chronological order. The first three books are like great stones or blocks that show Jesus Christ in 3D and they are very similar in the events covered. The last, the Gospel of John, is more like the mortar filling in the cracks. It's as if he, with the Spirit is saying, yeah that's all important and true, but here's something else you should know.

Matthew
28 chapters 1.5-2 hours to read

Chosen by Jesus to be one of the Twelve and walk with him Matthew, also called Levi, was placed first and his is the most quoted. Much is made of the fact that he collected taxes for the Romans, a job that was looked down on by the Jews; however, he did not go out and collect income tax. When the Romans took over a country, one of the first things they would do was to put in good roads. This would allow them to transfer troops and supplies quickly in case of an uprising, and merchants could also use them—for a fee of course. One of the heaviest traveled roads ran north and south through Judea by the Lake of Galilee. This is where Matthew worked and Jesus taught. Because his father's name, Alphaeus, is given it would likely mean his family was well-known and perhaps it is how he got a well-paying job at the toll booth. As a tax collector, he probably did not hang out with the other disciples but rather took off work whenever he could to go listen to Jesus preach. This is probably why he gives the most complete teaching of Jesus, at what is called the Sermon on the Mount. The fact that he wrote his Gospel first in Hebrew and then later in Greek, as the other Gospels were, as well as all of the references he makes to the prophecies and Tanakh or Old Testament show that his original audience was for the Jews, and it gives us a special insight as how the old and new flow together.

Chapters 1:1 thru 4:25   6-7 minutes to read

The genealogy and birth of Jesus; the Wise Men arrive and fleeing to Egypt. John the Baptist, the baptism and temptation of Jesus, the beginning of his ministry and choosing disciples.

Chapters 5:1 thru 7:29   10-13 minutes to read

The teachings of Christ in the Sermon on the Mount.

Chapters 8 thru 18:35   38-48 minutes to read

Jesus in Galilee, miracles, teaching, naming of the Twelve, parables, rejection by leaders, the death of John the Baptist. Jesus walks on the water, the transfiguration, teaching on discipline and forgiveness

Chapters 19:1 thru 20:34   6-8 minutes to read

Jesus travels to Jerusalem, he blesses children, a parable on the judgment, how to be truly great.

Chapters 21: thru 26:35   23-30 minutes to read

Jesus arrives in Jerusalem, the cleansing of the temple, disputes with the leaders, parables and teaching on the end of time. Judas makes a deal, the Last Supper.

Chapters 26:36 thru 28:20   11-14 minutes to read

Jesus in Gethsemane, his arrest and trials, Peter's denial, the death of Judas. Jesus is beaten and crucified, his tomb sealed and guarded. The resurrection, Jesus appears to the disciples, the Great Commission.

Mark

16 chapters 1-1:15 hours to read

It appears that John Mark was a boy, or young man, during the life of Jesus. Jesus and the disciples, as well as later on the Apostles, would often stay at what is referred to as his mother's house when in Jerusalem. This would mean that his family probably would also have been a successful one to have that large of a house and be able to take in that many people. Mark is often thought to be the young man in the Garden of Gethsemane who ran away when the soldiers arrested Jesus. Think of him as the young boy who was always hanging around in the shadows, catching everything going on, but not really being noticed. It seems that when older, but still young, Mark traveled with Peter, as well as his cousin Barnabas, along with Saul, spending quite a bit of time in Rome. His account is most likely written with the Romans in mind, as it puts emphasis on the power and mighty acts of Jesus, often described in detail. It's like the reporter's version: short and to the point.

Chapter 1:1 thru 1:13   1-2 minutes to read

The ministry of John the Baptist, the baptism and temptation of Jesus.

Chapters 1:14 thru 9:50   31-40 minutes to read

Healings, parables, the storm stilled, demons cast out, the Twelve sent out, the death of John the Baptist, feeding of thousands, walking on the water, disputes with leaders, and the transfiguration.

Chapter 10:1   5-6 minutes to read

Jesus travels to Jerusalem, his teaching on marriage, the rich young ruler, Jesus heals the blind.

Chapters 11:1 thru 14:32   14-17 minutes to read

Jesus arriving in Jerusalem, the cleansing of the temple, disputes with the leaders, three questions to trap Jesus and his responses, teaching on the end of time, Judas makes a deal, the Last Supper.

Chapters 14:33 thru 16:20   9-12 minutes to read

Jesus in Gethsemane, his arrest and trials, Jesus is mocked and crucified, the resurrection, his appearances, and ascension of Jesus into heaven.

Luke

24 Chapters   1:45-2:15 hours to read

The only writer in the whole of the Bible that came from Greece, and was most likely not a Jew. Luke was a physician writing to a believer with the title of a high-ranking Roman official. Luke also later wrote Acts to the same individual who no longer had the title, showing he had left the office by that point. Luke traveled a great deal with Paul and had also spent time in Jerusalem. Luke was not an eyewitness, which gives us a unique look at the life of Jesus as he wrote from the perspective of not just one person, but of many. Tradition has it that he spent a great deal of time with Mary the mother of Jesus and his brothers. This would give us a first-hand view of Jesus as a child and young man. Luke goes on to give us the testimony of all those Jesus healed and the hundreds of others who Jesus left a powerful impression on. All of them seeing so many of the same events, and **not just from the men** but no doubt also from the women who followed Jesus as well. Because of all who must of given input, it only makes sense that it is the longest of the Gospels. Jewish civilization was built around the Scriptures, Roman civilization around power and government, and the Greek civilization around philosophy, education, seeking wisdom, and beauty. The Gospel of Luke is often described as beautiful and well-written. He uses words and phrases the others do not and shows the wisdom and education of both himself and those he intended to reach.

Chapters 1:1 thru 4:13   16-20 minutes to read.

Introduction, birth and childhood of John the Baptist and Jesus, the ministry of John the Baptist, including the baptism of Jesus. The genealogy of Jesus, the temptation of Jesus in the wilderness.

Chapters 4:14 thru 9:50   28-34 minutes to read.

Jesus in Galilee, rejected in Nazareth, performing miracles, healings, the calling of disciples and choosing the Twelve, teaching and the Sermon on the Mount, parables, casting out demons, sending out the Twelve, the death of John the Baptist, the feeding of over five thousand, and the transfiguration.

Chapters 9:51 thru 19:27   39-49 minutes to read.

Going to Jerusalem, seventy disciples sent out ahead, teachings and warnings, healings, parables, the good Samaritan, the cost of following Jesus, the rich young ruler, and Zacchaeus.

Chapters 19:28 thru 22:38   13-16 minutes to read.

Entering Jerusalem, cleansing of the temple. Christ questioned and challenged, the end times and a call to always be ready, the Last Supper.

Chapters 22:39 thru 24:53   12-15 minutes to read

Jesus in Gethsemane, his betrayal, arrest, and, trials. Pilate tries to release Jesus, the two thieves on either side of Jesus, the crucifixion, the resurrection, Christ appears and teaches, and the ascension.

John

25 Chapters   1:25-1:45 hours to read

The mission of John the Baptist was to "make straight the way for the Lord." (John 1:23) While that includes preaching to the general population, I believe his greatest contribution was to prepare men to be disciples of Jesus right out of the gate. John the apostle and writer, his brother James, as well as Simon Peter and his brother Andrew, are among that group. With Jesus from the beginning, not only were they among the first, but they were also the closest. You find them with Jesus on occasions when the others stayed behind. John was the son of Zebedee, devout, well-known, and head of a successful family of fishermen that had employees, or "servants," and partnered with Peter. John also had a house in Jerusalem, and when Jesus was arrested, he was so well-known to the servants of the high priest that he was let in without question and was able to bring Peter in as well. Jesus called John and James "Sons of Thunder," which shows they like Peter were not shy but rather bold in speech and actions. They were the kind of men that it would take to be, as Paul would later describe them, "Pillars of the Church." (Gal 2: 9-10) John was the only one of the Twelve who did not suffer a martyr's death but lived to an old age, also writing 1st, 2nd, and 3rd John as well as Revelation. Tradition has it that later in life he made his home at Ephesus.

Chapters 1:1 thru 6:71   25-32 minutes to read.

Jesus' true nature, introduction of John the Baptist, the first disciples called, the first miracle, the first cleansing of the temple. Jesus and Nicodemus, the woman at the well, healings and teachings, thousands fed, Jesus walks on water, Jesus is the bread of life, yet many do not understand and go away.

Chapters 7:1 thru 12:11   24-30 minutes to read.

Teaching at the Feast of Tabernacles, a woman caught in adultery, Jesus confronts unbelievers, a man born blind is healed and questioned by the leaders, teachings and division among the Jews, Lazarus is raised from the dead, the plot to kill Jesus, Jesus is anointed by Mary of Bethany.

Chapters 12:12 thru 12:50   4-5 minutes to read.

Jesus enters Jerusalem for the last time, teaching on what is about to happen and his authority.

Chapters 13:1 thru 17:26   16-20 minutes to read.

Jesus teaches in the upper room, washing of the disciples feet, the Last Supper, Judas leaves them, Jesus tells them he is leaving and about the coming of the Holy Spirit. His prayer to be glorified, for the disciples, and all of us who come later.

Chapter 18:1 thru 21:25   15-19 minutes to read.

Jesus in the Garden of Gethsemane, his arrest and trials, Jesus is beaten, mocked and crucified. The resurrection, his appearances at the tomb, in a closed room, to Thomas, and by the shore. Jesus questions Peter, closing remarks.

Acts of the Apostles
28 Chapters   1:45-2:10 hours to read

Written by Luke, Acts is a continuation of the story of Jesus and the beginning of the church. It starts with the ascension of Jesus into heaven and ends with Paul, who is still preaching Jesus although he is now a prisoner in Rome. Just as the Gospels cover a thirty to thirty-five year period, Acts covers the next thirty to thirty-five years. It covers the story of the followers of Jesus as they go from a small group to a worldwide following that will last to the end of time. Every example of the "plan of salvation" put into action, meaning people coming to the knowledge of Jesus and being saved, is found in Acts. Luke was an eyewitness to most of what he wrote, using terms such as us and we. The main characters are Peter and Paul, with most of the letter containing the travels of Paul as he spread the Gospel to a world that for the most part is immoral and has little to no understanding of the true God.

Chapters 1:1 thru 6:7   19-21 minutes to read.

Introduction, Jesus lifted into heaven, the Holy Spirit fills the Apostles, the first sermon, and the beginning of the church. The persecution begins and the church grows, the first deacons appointed.

Chapters 6:8 thru 11:18   20-26 minutes to read.

The first Martyr, examples of conversions. Jesus appears to Saul, and he is baptized then changes his name to Paul. Peter heals and raises the dead, and the church is opened to the whole world.

Chapters 11:19 thru 12:25   4-5 minutes to read.

The persecution intensifies, believers leave Jerusalem, and so the Gospel spreads with them. Barnabas and Saul preach to the Greeks in Antioch, James the apostle is martyred, Peter is arrested and freed by an angel, Herod dies.

Chapters 13:1 thru 15:35   11-14 minutes to read.

Barnabas and Saul are called to be missionaries and set out. Some Jews want the Gentles to be circumcised; after a debate, Peter speaks and the whole church agrees rejecting the idea.

Chapters 15:36 thru 18:22   10-13 minutes to read.

Barnabas and Paul separate. Barnabas takes Mark, and Paul takes Silas; Timothy joins them.

Chapters 18:23 thru 21:16   10-13 minutes to read.

Paul's third missionary journey. Apollos, a powerful speaker, is taught about the baptism into Jesus.

Chapters 21:17 thru 28:31   27-34 minutes to read.

Paul is arrested and gives defense in Jerusalem and Caesarea. He is then shipwrecked on the way to Rome but arrives safe and begins to preach there while in custody.

Examples of people being saved: The first Gospel sermon, Acts 2:37-41—Simon the sorcerer, 8:5-13—The Ethiopian eunuch, 8:35-39—Cornelius, the first gentile, 10:34-48—Lydia, 16:13-15—The jailer and his household, 16:31-34 and Saul who changes his name to Paul, 22:10-18

The Letters of Paul

Paul was born Saul in the city of Tarsus, which was an academic city, considered to be third in the known world at that time. He was a devout Jew, well-educated, and a member of the Pharisees. He was also born a Roman citizen, which was very rare. Convinced Christianity was destroying Judaism, he would travel with soldiers to arrest Christians and put them in jail, where they could face death. It was while he was on the

road to Damascus, for just such a purpose, that Jesus appeared
to him in a bright light. After both seeing and talking to Jesus
Saul was left blind until Ananias, who was sent by the Lord,
came and touched him. He was immediately healed and then
baptized into Jesus. Saul was like one of those wind-up toy
soldiers that marches full speed into a wall then turns and
then marches full speed in the other direction. It was when
he changed directions that he changed his name to Paul. We
know quite a bit about him because Luke traveled with him,
and wrote about the experience. Paul traveled the country,
preaching Jesus to Jews and Gentiles alike; however, it was
with the Gentiles that he had the most success. Because he was
traveling, he would often write letters to the churches, most of
which he had started. He also wrote to give instruction to the
young men he had taught. He was finally arrested in Jerusalem
and sent to Rome, where he continued to write and preach
until he was put to death, probably by Nero. Of the twenty-
seven books of the New Testament, thirteen are from Paul. He
spoke and wrote with power from the Spirit of GOD, and his
letters give us powerful insight as to how we connect and walk
with the Almighty.

Romans
16 Chapters   41-51 minutes to read

Chapters 1:1 thru 3:20   7-9 minutes to read.
   Introduction, all are guilty before God.

Chapters 3:21 thru 8:39   14-18 minutes to read.

No one is able to earn salvation; it is only through Christ Jesus. Although we fail, we have a sure hope. When we set our minds on things of the Spirit, all things work together for good.

Chapters 9:1 thru 11:36   8-10 minutes to read.

The failing of the Jews is not God's fault; just as they can be cut off, so Gentiles can be grafted in. Only a remnant will be saved; it is not by birth but rather a decision.

Chapters 12:1 thru 15:33   9-11 minutes to read.

How a Christian is to conduct themselves in everything, closing remarks.

Chapter 16:1   2-3 minutes to read.

A note to Ephesus included with the letter to Rome, greetings, avoid those that create dissensions.

First Corinthians
6 Chapters   40-53 minutes to read

Chapter 1:1 thru 7:48   16-20 minutes to read.

Factions in the church, a call for unity, grow in the Spirit, humble yourself, both Paul and Apollos are servants of God, not competitors. Sexual immorality in the church, drive out wickedness, lawsuits, principles of marriage.

Chapters 8 thru 11:1   7-9 minutes to read.

Life in a pagan society, freedoms, and restrictions.

Chapters 11:2 thru 16:24   18-24 minutes to read.

Public worship, the resurrection is the foundation of faith, the nature of the resurrection, closing remarks.

Second Corinthians
13 Chapters   28-35 minutes to read

A review and defense of his past relation with the church and a call for separation from the world. Titus is coming to pick up a collection for the saints in need; they are warned about false teachers who have come in, and he defends himself and teaching. A call to examine themselves and change their ways before he returns again.

Galatians
6 Chapters   14-18 minutes to read

Paul is an apostle from God, not from man, they have accepted false teachers, he tells his story of how he came to Jesus. We are not slaves that have to work to be paid, but sons and heirs. The threat of legalism, walk in freedom by the Spirit, avoid the desires of the flesh, don't be deceived, we sow what we reap, do good to all.

Ephesians
6 Chapters   13-17 minutes to read

What God has done for us, or what we have received: the riches of his grace and mercy. What we are to do in response, how we must act, be separate from and not like the world, directions for the Christian family, put on the armor of God.

Philippians

4 Chapters   10-13 minutes to read

Thanksgiving and joy both for, and to them. Even though he is imprisoned it has served to spread the Gospel. Be worthy of Christ our model, shine like a light in a perverse world, he is sending Timothy to them, watch for false teachers, forgetting what is past look forward to the goal, rejoice in the Lord always, and think on these things. God supplies all needs.

Colossians

4 Chapters   9-11 minutes to read

His prayer for them. Christ the foundation and fullness of God. Let no one prey on you by philosophy, deceit, tradition, and spirits of the universe, you put on Christ in baptism, let no one pass judgment on you, set your minds on things above. Put to death what is earthly, put on the ways of love. Instructions for the Christian family, continue in prayer, be wise, closing.

First Thessalonians

5 Chapters   9-12 minutes to read

Paul's joy over the way they received the Gospel, and the news he has received about them. A call to purity and an upright life, find comfort in the resurrection, test everything, abstain from every form of evil.

Second Thessalonians

3 Chapters   5-6 minutes to read

He gives thanks for their faith, a call to endure, teaching about the end of time. God will send a strong delusion, stand firm, do not be idle and stay away from those who are.

Paul's Letters to Timothy

Paul met the young man Timothy on his second missionary journey just after he and Barnabas had decided to go separate ways. Timothy's father was Greek, and his mother was Jewish. He was taught by his mother and grandmother and was a believer with a solid reputation when he met Paul and began to travel with him. Paul thought of him as his "true child" in the faith and often had him stay behind, or travel to cities to help the young churches. He was imprisoned at least once and released. Tradition has it that he spent his latter years in Ephesus, where John was as well, and that he was eventually martyred.

First Timothy

6 Chapters   10-13 minutes to read

Urge believers to stay away from speculations and vain discussions, pray for people in authority, a woman's position in the church, qualifications for being a bishop, a deacon, a deaconess. Watch out for false teaching and myths, teach godliness in speech and conduct, treat believers of all ages as you would family, instruction for widows, honor elders, and instructions for workers and the rich. Many are divisive and greedy; as for you stay steadfast.

Second Timothy

4 Chapters   7-9 minutes to read

We have a spirit of power and self-control, do not be ashamed of testifying, avoid disputes over words, rightly handle the word of truth, people will turn away in the last days, know the Scripture so you will be complete, preach, convince, rebuke, extort, be patient in teaching. The time of his departure has come. Paul urges Timothy to come before winter and bring Mark. Many have left, but Luke is still with him.

Titus

Titus traveled with Paul, and like Timothy Paul called him a "true child" in a common faith. Titus was Greek, so unlike Timothy Paul resisted having him circumcised. He was sent to Corinth, where the church was having problems as we know from 1st Corinthians. Then he stayed behind in Crete, where he received this letter, and where similar problems existed. He must have been a bold and strong Christian, able to deal with those who wander from the Gospel into secular thinking. In this letter Paul asked him to come to Greece, where he was spending the winter, after he was replaced by someone Paul would send. Tradition has it that he returned to Crete later in life, where he served as an Elder and died peacefully.

3 Chapters   4-5 minutes to read

Qualifications for church leaders, expose false teachers, a description of sound doctrine. Admonish someone who is divisive once or twice, then have nothing to do with them.

Philemon

1 Chapter   2-3 minutes to read

An appeal for a runaway slave who became a believer and is now returning to his owner, Philemon. The Bible does not condone nor condemn slavery; it merely acknowledges it exists. I suppose if the Kingdom of Christ was of this world it would be different. Instead, Christ simply directs all of us to act out of love to one other in every situation we find ourselves in.

Hebrews

There is no indication of who the author is. Because Paul wrote so many letters and Timothy is mentioned, it is natural to think of him first. However, there are some real discrepancies in writing style additionally the author states he is not an eyewitness but learned from those who were. Whoever the author was, he was dedicated, educated, and well-versed in the Tanakh, or Old Testament Scriptures. He had no doubt spent considerable time preaching Jesus to the Jewish nation, as this was clearly not his first attempt at reaching out to them. The conclusion indicates he was writing to believers, which means he was both strengthening them and instructing them on how to reach fellow Jews. To the rest of us, it gives us the background to understand how the old law brought forward the new covenant. Just as the Hebrews were chosen, and were born into a relationship with GOD, so all of us are also chosen when we are born into what is an even closer relationship with GOD through Jesus in the Spirit.

13 Chapters   29-36 minutes to read

Jesus is superior to the angels, superior to Moses and Joshua, and superior to the priesthood as God made him high priest forever. The new covenant of Christ is superior to the old, Christ was the superior one-time sacrifice for sin, a call to hold firm. Faith is defined, the example of faith in those who came before, stand firm in faith, do not reject the discipline of the Father, stand in reverence and awe, and act accordingly. Jesus Christ is the same yesterday today and forever, to him be the glory forever and ever.

James

Traditionally, the writer has always been identified as James, Jesus's brother. Jesus had four brothers as well as sisters. (Mt 1:55) James was married, (1 Cor 9:5) a leader of the church in Jerusalem, (Acts 15:13, 21:18) and Jesus appeared to him after his resurrection. (1 Cor 15:7) Tradition gives three stories of his death; according to all three, he was stoned. One adds that he was first thrown down from a balcony of the temple after he had been told to cry out that Jesus was not the Christ, and he did just the opposite. Then he was finally clubbed to death after being stoned.

5 Chapters   10-13 minutes to read

True religion, evidenced by enduring trials and one's conduct. True faith, evidenced by impartiality, by works, and by words. True wisdom is from above, separate from the world. Do not slander or take an oath, we can't see tomorrow, know that the reign of the rich will end, so be patient and pray in everything.

Peter

Originally named Simon, the first thing Jesus did when they met was to change his name to Peter, which means "rock," or a piece of one. (Jn.1:42) Among the first disciples of Jesus he was part of the inner circle of disciples, and later the Twelve, along with John. Whenever the Apostles are listed his name always appears first. Like John, he was a fisherman and was in business with John's family (Lk. 5:10) The one thing that stands out about him, is that he was always quick to speak. Peter was married (Mt. 8:14) and his wife went with him when he later traveled preaching. (1 Cor. 9:5) After the resurrection, Jesus told him he would be martyred, and whether true or not, tradition has it he was crucified upside down so as not to die the same way Jesus did.

First Peter

5 Chapters   10-13 minutes to read

The blessings of Christ, who Christ is, what he has done, and who we are when in him. How we are to act toward unbelievers, the government, at work, our spouse, in persecution,

163

in the world. Be faithful and humble in trials, use your gifts, God will take your worries and give you strength.

Second Peter

3 Chapters   7-9 minutes to read

How to grow in power and knowledge. There are false teachers, their conduct, and the consequences. Christ is coming again, the heavens and earth will be dissolved, the ignorant and unstable twist the Scriptures, beware, and grow in grace and knowledge.

First John

5 Chapters   11-14 minutes to read

John was an eyewitness. The test of righteousness, love, and true belief. Put obedience, love, and belief in action. Faith overcomes the world and gives life. Know that you have eternal life, God hears you, God keeps you. In the world is the power of evil, but the Son of God gives us truth and life.

Second John

1 Chapter   2-3 minutes to read

The commandment of love, there are many deceivers, do not receive nor even greet them.

Third John

1 Chapter   2-3 minutes to read

A personal letter praising those who follow the truth and upbraiding one who puts himself first.

Jude

"Jude, a servant of Jesus Christ and a brother of James," (Jude 1:1). This statement makes it all the more likely that the two writers (James and Jude) are the same listed in Mt. 13:55 as the physical brothers of Jesus. He is listed last, so it is also likely he is the youngest.

1 Chapter   3-4 minutes to read

The character and fate of false teachers: they are worldly, divisive, and without the Spirit. God through Jesus Christ is able to keep you from falling, and without blemish.

Revelation

22 Chapters   50-65 minutes to read

Written by John the Apostle, this is a revelation that he had when he was an old man about the end of time, and the judgment to follow. It is written in figurative language, and while it can be interesting to read, it is for the most part, hard to understand and interpret. However, as you would expect, the end is very powerful.

Chapters 1 thru 3:22   9-12 minutes to read.
Introduction, messages to the seven churches.

Chapters 4 thru 20:10   35-44 minutes to read.
That which is to come, seven seals, seven trumpets, seven figures, seven bowls, judgment of Babylon, the defeat of the

beast and the false prophet, the binding of Satan, the thousand year reign of Christ, Satan is loosed.

Chapters 20:11 thru 22:21   6-8 minutes to read.

The Judgment, a new heaven and new earth, a new Jerusalem. An invitation and warning to all.

Appendix

Sometime around 1,400BC in Gen 3:15 Moses wrote about the fall from grace and sin coming into the world. It was then that GOD declared that evil would continue to exist but that he would send one born of a woman and that while his heel would be bruised he would crush the head of the one that brought evil and sin into the world. And so it starts...

OT – is from the Old Testament

NT – is from the New Testament

1)[1] In 740 to700 BC a forerunner was foretold.

OT – "A voice of one calling: "In the wilderness prepare the way for the Lord; make straight in the desert a highway for our God." (Isa 40:3)

NT – "Who are you? Give us an answer to take back to those who sent us. What do you say about yourself?" John replied in the words of Isaiah the prophet, "I am the voice of one calling in the wilderness, 'Make straight the way for the Lord.'" (John 1:23)

2) In 740 to 700 BC It is even foretold that he would be born of a virgin.

OT – "Therefore the Lord himself will give you a sign: The virgin will be with child and will give birth to a son, and will call him Immanuel[a]." (Isa 7:14) Which translated means "With us is God"

NT – "The angel answered, "The Holy Spirit will come on you, and the power of the Most High will overshadow you. So the holy one to be born will be called the Son of God." (Luke 1:35)

3)[2] Around 800 to 700BC we find that he would be born in Bethlehem.

OT – "But you, Bethlehem Ephrathah, though you are small among the clans of Judah, out of you will come for me one who will be ruler over Israel, whose origins are from of old, from ancient times." (Mic 5:2)

NT – "After Jesus was born in Bethlehem in Judea, during the time of King Herod" (Matt 2:1)

4) In 760 to 720BC We find he will be called out of Egypt.

OT – "...out of Egypt I called my son." (Hos 11:1)

NT – "...an angel of the Lord appeared to Joseph in a dream. "Get up," he said, "take the child and his mother and escape to Egypt. Stay there until I tell you, for Herod is going to search for the child to kill him." So he got up, took the child and his mother during the night and left for Egypt, where he stayed until the death of Herod." (Matt 2:13-15)

5) In 740 to 700 BC we are told he will reside and teach in the land of Galilee.

   OT – "In the past he humbled the land of Zebulun and the land of Naphtali, but in the future he will honor Galilee of the nations, by the Way of the Sea, beyond the Jordan" (Isa 9:1)

   NT – "When Jesus heard that John had been put in prison, he returned to Galilee. Leaving Nazareth, he went and lived in Capernaum, which was by the lake in the area of Zebulun and Naphtali" (Matt 4:12-13)

6) In 1010 to 930 BC we see the one from God will speak in parables.

   OT – "I will open my mouth with a parable; I will utter hidden things, things from of old" (Ps 78:2)

   NT – "Jesus spoke all these things to the crowd in parables; he did not say anything to them without using a parable." (Matt 13:34-35)

7) In 740 to 700 BC we find that people will hear but not understand.

   OT – "Be ever hearing, but never understanding; be ever seeing, but never perceiving.' (Isa 6:9)

   NT – "Though seeing, they do not see; though hearing, they do not hear or understand." (Matt 13:13)

8) Also in 740 to 700 BC we are told he will be rejected.

   OT – "He was despised and rejected by mankind...and we held him in low esteem." (Isa 53:3)

NT – "They got up, drove him out of the town, and took him to the brow of the hill on which the town was built, in order to throw him off the cliff. But he walked right through the crowd and went on his way."(Luke 4:29-30)

9)³ In 520 to 518 BC we find he will ride into Jerusalem on a donkey.

OT – "Rejoice greatly, O Daughter Zion! Shout, Daughter Jerusalem! See, your king comes to you, righteous and victorious, lowly and riding on a donkey, on a colt, the foal of a donkey." (Zech 9:9)

NT – "As they approached Jerusalem...Jesus sent two disciples, saying to them, "Go to the village ahead of you, and at once you will find a donkey tied there, with her colt by her...They brought the donkey and the colt, and placed their cloaks on them, for Jesus to sit on." (Matt 21:1-7)

10)⁴ In 1010 to 930 BC we are told he would be betrayed by a close friend he had broke bread with.

OT – "Even my close friend, someone I trusted, one who shared my bread, has turned against me." (Ps 41:9)

NT – "Very truly I tell you one of you is going to betray me."... "It is the one to whom I will give this piece of bread when I have dipped it in the dish." Then, dipping the piece of bread, he gave it to Judas, the son of Simon Iscariot" (John" 13:21-26)

11) ⁵&⁶ In 520 to 518 BC not only was he to be betrayed for thirty pieces of silver but the money was to go to a potter as well.

OT – "So they paid me thirty pieces of silver...And the Lord said to me, "Throw it to the potter"-the handsome price at which they valued me!" (Zech 11:12-13)

NT – "When Judas, who had betrayed him, saw that Jesus was condemned, he was seized with remorse and returned the thirty pieces of silver to the chief priests and the elders... They decided to use the money to buy the potter's field as a burial place for foreigners." (Matt 27:3, 7)

12) [7] In 740 to 700 It was foretold he would not make a defense.

OT – "He was oppressed and afflicted, yet he did not open his mouth; he was led like a lamb to the slaughter, and as a sheep before her shearers is silent, so he did not open his mouth." (Isa 53:7)

NT – "Then the high priest stood up and said to Jesus,"Are you not going to answer? What is this testimony that these men are bringing against you?" But Jesus remained silent." (Matt 26:62-63)

13) [8] Clear back in 1010 to 930 BC we see how Jesus is to die, that no bones will be broken, and that they will cast lots for his clothes.

OT – "A band of evil men has encircled me, they have pierced my hands and my feet. I can count all my bones; people stare and gloat over me. They divide my garments among them and cast lots for my clothing." (Ps 22:16-18)

NT – "When they had crucified him, they divided up his

clothes by casting lots. And sitting down, they kept watch over him there." (Matt 27:35-36)

14) Also back in 1010 to 930 BC we are told he would be raised from the dead.

OT – "You will not abandon me to the realm of the dead, nor will you let your faithful one see decay." (Ps 16:10)

NT – "Seeing what was to come, he (King David) spoke of the resurrection of the Messiah, that he was not abandoned to the realm of the dead, nor did his body see decay. God has raised this Jesus to life, and we are all witnesses of it." (Acts 2:31-32)

15) In 605 BC a New Covenant is promised.

OT – "The days are coming," declares the Lord,"when I will make a new covenant" (Jer 31:31)

NT – (Jesus said) "This is my blood of the covenant, which is poured out for many for the forgiveness of sins." (Matt 26:28)

16) In 520 to 518 we are told it will not be just for a nation but that it will cover the entire world and last forever.

OT – "His rule will extend from sea to sea and from the River to the ends of the earth." (Zech 9:10)

NT – "Therefore go and make disciples of all nations, baptizing them in the name of the Father and of the Son and of the Holy Spirit, and teaching them to obey everything I have commanded you. And surely I am with you always, to the very end of the age." (Matt 28:19-20)

[1-8] A often-quoted math professor[1] some years ago had twelve classes with around 600 students total figure the probability of just these eight references coming true. After adjusting the numbers to be on the conservative side they came up with 1- 10^{17} and then had it peer reviewed. If with the same odds of these eight, you were to increase the number of references to sixteen it would become 1-10^{45}, forty-eight references would be 1-10^{157} that's a 1 with 157 zeros behind it! That's just for forty-eight, keep in mind there are between sixty to over three hundred of them. Many of them are such that a person could not cause it to come about even if they were to attempt it. Some are such that a skeptic would take issue with, however, even if you were to take issue with the numbers and references and reduce them by 30, 40, or even 50 percent, the odds are still way beyond any chance of a coincidence. When odds get that high impossibility is something that has sparked the interest of both mathematicians and philosophers alike.

A French mathematician named Emile Borel wrote several papers, one of which has become known as "Borel's Law." It states that events with a probability on the scale of 1 in 10^{50} simply will not happen. They are impossible. While often used when discussing creation, the argument against it is that it does not take time into effect, making creation layer upon layer of very high odds that have many centuries

---

[1] Peter Stoner, *Science Speaks* (Chicago: Moody Publishing, 1958)

to occur. Which, by the way, he argues in a separate paper, that when that happens they will always remain very high. Also keep in mind, they still would have to happen in just the right order. However, that is not the case with the life of Jesus; in fact, some of the prophecies themselves have to do with time. You can take it as a scientific fact, with higher odds than perhaps even creation itself, that Jesus came from GOD and is exactly who the Bible says he is.

To order books, artwork, or send an email visit:

The-Way.online

There are many people around you that the only way they will learn to walk in The Way is through you. You are their best, and maybe only hope. Knowing what to say and when to say it is hard. Handing them a copy of this book is easy. It is an inexpensive way for you to help others, spread the Gospel, and make sure there are others in heaven because of you.

About the Author

The author is a sinner. He gave his life to GOD over sixty years ago and has failed him ever since. No matter his intentions or how hard he has tried he has let people down; he has said and done the wrong thing more times than you can count. He is in no way worthy of GOD's grace, and yet the Spirit continues to guide him in love. The LORD has brought into his life some of the finest teachers ever placed on this earth that you've never heard of, and he stands in their shadows. He has taught, preached, and led with limited success to a number of churches for many years. Pay attention when you read; you should not believe him without checking every Scripture to make sure it was not taken out of context, and that his words accurately describe what the Bible is teaching. If they do, then integrate them into your life, and everything up to that point was well worth it. The best thing about this book is that if it inspires or helps you in any way to draw closer to GOD you know it came through the Holy Spirit and not the author. May you be blessed and guided by reading and walking in *The Way*.